Basel

Travel Guide 2025

A Local's Perspective on Basel's History, Markets, and Must-See Attractions

Melissa A. Jackson

Copyright © 2025 Melissa A. Jackson

All rights reserved. No part of this publication may be reproduced, distributed, or transmitted in any form or by any means, including photocopying, recording, or other electronic or mechanical methods, without the prior written permission of the publisher, except in the case of brief quotations embodied in critical reviews and certain other non-commercial uses permitted by copyright law.

- Introduction to Basel 6
  - History and Cultural Significance 10
  - Why Basel is a Must-Visit Destination 12
  - The Basel Experience 17
- Planning Your Trip 22
  - Best Time to Visit Basel 22
  - Visa Requirements and Entry Information 24
  - Health and Safety Tips for Travelers 27
  - Currency, Banking, and Local Tips 32
  - Local Language 36
  - Emergency Contacts and Important Information 38
- Accommodation in Basel 42
- Getting to and Around Basel 53
- Museums and Galleries 61
  - Overview of Basel's Vibrant Art Scene 61
  - Must-Visit Museums and Galleries 65
  - Specialized Art Spaces and Exhibitions 70
  - Exploring Contemporary Art in Basel 74
- Shopping in Basel 78
- Hidden Gems in Basel 84

    Secret Courtyards and Alleys 84

    Lesser-Known Museums and Art Spaces 87

    Unusual Spots for Art and History Enthusiasts 92

    Lesser-Known Parks and Green Spaces 97

    Quiet Cafes and Unique Spots to Relax 101

Nightlife and Entertainment 107

    Basel's Vibrant Nightlife Scene 107

    Live Music Venues and Jazz Clubs 109

    Evening Events and Festivals 111

    Late-Night Dining and Snacks 114

Family-Friendly Activities 117

    Fun for All Ages 117

    Kid-Friendly Museums and Educational Spots 119

    Parks and Playgrounds for Children 122

    Fun Outdoor Activities for Families 125

    Family-Friendly Dining Options 128

    Day Trips and Attractions Suitable for Families 130

Day Trips from Basel 134

    Best Nearby Destinations for a Day Trip 134

    Exploring the Countryside and Nearby Villages 137

Adventure and Nature Day Trips from Basel 140
River Cruises and Scenic Train Routes 144
Exploring Neighboring Countries 147
Conclusion 150

Introduction to Basel

Arriving in Basel

Basel doesn't announce itself with grand gestures. It's a city that moves at its own pace, confident in what it offers without demanding attention. Arriving at the EuroAirport, the efficiency was noticeable. Despite sitting on the borders of France, Germany, and Switzerland, crossing into the Swiss side felt effortless. The Basel Card, given to every overnight visitor, made public transport free and straightforward, eliminating any concerns about getting around. The tram system is well-connected, punctual, and clean, a contrast to many major cities where transit is often a compromise rather than a convenience.

Walking Through the Old Town

The Old Town is where Basel quietly reveals its layers of history. Unlike other European cities that rely on grand squares and towering landmarks, Basel's charm lies in the details. The cobbled streets curve unpredictably, lined with medieval buildings that don't feel like museum pieces but rather functioning parts of the city. The Münster stands tall with its red sandstone and twin spires, yet it isn't the most striking part. The cloistered courtyard behind it has a different presence—quiet, removed from the city's movement, allowing time to settle. The Pfalz terrace just beyond it opens up to a panoramic view of the Rhine. Standing there, the river's current is visible, unhurried yet constant, moving with a rhythm that defines Basel itself.

The Role of the Rhine

The Rhine is not just a geographical feature but a part of everyday life. It's an active space where locals swim in summer, letting the river carry them downstream while their belongings float beside them in waterproof bags. During colder months, the banks become an extension of the city's rhythm, with cyclists, walkers, and café-goers using the space at a natural, unforced pace. The river ferries, driven purely by the current, are more than a mode of transport. They are a reminder of how Basel embraces practicality without stripping away character.

Art as a Constant

Art is not confined to museums in Basel; it exists in the city's structure. The Kunstmuseum holds an impressive collection, yet what makes it remarkable is the understated way these masterpieces are displayed. There's no excessive signage or forced narratives—just art, positioned for those who want to see it. Fondation Beyeler, slightly outside the city, has a different atmosphere. The space itself influences the experience, with large windows that bring in natural light, making the art feel less removed from the real world. Even outside the institutions, art spills onto the streets in the form of murals, installations, and sculptures, blending seamlessly into daily life rather than feeling like curated attractions.

Food Without Pretense

Basel's food scene does not chase trends. Traditional Swiss influences remain strong, but the city's location ensures that

French and German elements filter in naturally. The old guild houses serve meals that feel rooted in history—uncomplicated yet precise. Eating at one of these establishments means experiencing Basel's past through its flavors, with dishes that have been served for generations. At the other end of the spectrum, a simple bratwurst from a street vendor captures the city's practical approach to food. There's an appreciation for quality without the need for embellishment.

Evenings in Basel

Basel does not transform at night. There is no drastic shift in energy, no attempt to become something it isn't. Instead, the evenings maintain the same balanced pace, with bars and restaurants filling up just enough to create a sense of presence without overwhelming. Locals gather in small groups, conversations unfolding naturally over drinks. The absence of excessive noise or spectacle gives the city an understated liveliness—one that doesn't demand participation but welcomes it for those who choose to stay.

History and Cultural Significance

Basel's history dates back to Roman times, and its strategic location on the banks of the Rhine River has played a significant role in its growth and development. Originally established as a Roman settlement in the 1st century AD, Basel grew over time into a vital city within the Holy Roman Empire. Its geographical position at the crossroads of three countries—Switzerland, France, and Germany—allowed it to become an important center for trade, culture, and politics.

In the Middle Ages, Basel gained prominence as a religious and intellectual hub. The establishment of the University of Basel in 1460 marked a major milestone, positioning the city as a center for education and scholarship in Europe. The university attracted scholars from across the continent, and its influence extended into the realms of religion, with Basel playing a pivotal role during the Reformation. Notably, Erasmus of Rotterdam, a key figure of the period, was associated with the university, which further cemented the city's role in shaping the intellectual climate of the time.

Basel's commercial significance grew in tandem with its educational and religious influence. During the 14th and 15th centuries, it became an important trading hub, particularly in the textile industry. This economic prosperity set the stage for Basel's development as a financial center, a role it continues to play in modern times. The city's banking institutions have made it one of Switzerland's economic powerhouses.

In the 16th century, Basel's alignment with the Protestant Reformation distinguished it from other Swiss cities. As a Protestant stronghold, the city's religious institutions shifted in response to the Reformation's influence. The Basel Munster, with its striking architecture, became a symbol of Basel's Protestant heritage, marking the city as a key player in the religious transformation sweeping through Europe.

Basel's cultural impact extends beyond religion and education to the arts. The city has long been a haven for artists and musicians, with the Basel School of Art, founded in the 19th century, encouraging creative expression. Basel's prominence in the global art world is evident through Art Basel, the internationally renowned contemporary art fair that draws artists, collectors, and art enthusiasts from around the world. This event reinforces Basel's role as a cultural leader, positioning it as one of the foremost destinations for contemporary art.

Additionally, Basel is home to a range of important cultural institutions, such as the Kunstmuseum, which houses works from artists like Picasso, van Gogh, and Cézanne. These museums, along with Basel's commitment to maintaining a balance between preserving its history and embracing modern artistic movements, contribute to its distinct cultural identity.

Why Basel is a Must-Visit Destination

Rich Historical Significance

Basel has a long and deep-rooted history, which is evident in its landmarks and culture. As a city with origins dating back to Roman times, its role in trade, education, and religion has shaped its identity over centuries. The Old Town of Basel preserves its medieval charm, with narrow streets and centuries-old buildings, offering visitors a tangible connection to its past. The University of Basel, founded in 1460, adds to the city's historical significance, continuing to be an important academic institution. The Basel Munster, with its striking architecture, represents the city's role in the Protestant Reformation and is a key part of its historical landscape.

Vibrant Arts and Culture Scene

Basel stands out in the art world, particularly for its contemporary art scene. Art Basel, one of the most prestigious international art fairs, draws visitors from around the world, cementing the city's reputation as an art hub. The Kunstmuseum holds a vast collection of art from renowned figures such as Picasso, van Gogh, and Cézanne, making it a must-see for art lovers. Basel is also home to modern art venues like Fondation Beyeler, where visitors can experience a balance of historical and contemporary works. This rich cultural environment makes Basel a key destination for those interested in the arts.

Strategic Location

Basel is uniquely located at the intersection of Switzerland, France, and Germany. This geographical advantage makes it easy for travelers to explore nearby countries, as it serves as a gateway for cross-border travel. The city is well-connected by rail and air, making it a convenient starting point for regional travel. Visitors can explore the picturesque regions along the Rhine River or venture into neighboring countries for a diverse travel experience. Basel's strategic location, combined with its efficient public transport system, makes it easy to move around and access nearby attractions.

Cultural Festivals

Basel is known for its rich cultural events, with the Basler Fasnacht being one of the city's most celebrated festivals. This carnival, held annually, is a unique blend of parades, street performances, and elaborate costumes. It reflects the city's community spirit and deep cultural roots. Thousands of visitors flock to Basel each year to witness this lively event, which is a significant part of the local culture. It offers travelers a chance to experience Basel's traditions in an immersive and vibrant way.

Diverse Culinary Scene

Basel's culinary offerings reflect the city's location at the crossroads of Switzerland, France, and Germany. The city features a variety of dining options, from high-end restaurants offering French-inspired dishes to street vendors serving traditional Swiss fare. Basel is particularly known for its chocolates, local pastries, and craft beer scene, all of which showcase the region's rich culinary heritage. The city also boasts a growing wine culture, with local vineyards producing wine varieties that visitors can taste at restaurants and local bars.

Walkable and Compact City

Basel is a highly walkable city, with many of its key attractions, such as museums, historic sites, and the Rhine River, all within easy walking distance. This compact layout makes it an ideal destination for travelers who prefer exploring on foot. Whether strolling through the Old Town or visiting one of the many museums, walking around Basel allows visitors to take in the city's relaxed atmosphere at a comfortable pace. The pedestrian-friendly streets and open spaces enhance the city's appeal, offering a more intimate and leisurely travel experience.

Unique Architecture

Basel offers an interesting mix of old and new architecture. The city's medieval buildings, such as the Basel Munster and its city gates, stand in contrast to modern structures like the Vitra Campus and the contemporary buildings housing its museums. This combination of architectural styles gives Basel a distinctive character, where visitors can appreciate both the city's rich historical past and its modern, forward-thinking approach to design. The architectural diversity adds another layer of interest to Basel, making it a visually stimulating place to visit.

The Basel Experience

Artistic Legacy

Basel's status as an art capital is undeniable. The city has long been a hub for both historical and contemporary art, with world-class institutions like the Kunstmuseum and Fondation Beyeler. These museums house works from some of history's most celebrated artists, including Picasso, van Gogh, and Cézanne. But Basel's connection to the art world extends beyond museums. The globally renowned Art Basel fair draws art collectors, artists, and enthusiasts from around the world, reinforcing the city's place at the center of the global art scene. Visitors can explore a range of exhibitions, installations, and galleries that reflect Basel's innovative spirit in the arts.

Historical Significance

Basel's rich history is an integral part of its identity. The city dates back to Roman times and played a significant role during the Middle Ages and the Reformation. Key historical landmarks such as the Basel Munster, a stunning cathedral with origins from the 12th century, highlight the city's religious and architectural history. The University of Basel, founded in 1460, is one of Europe's oldest universities, which has continually contributed to the city's intellectual and cultural life. Basel's historic Old Town is another draw, offering visitors a glimpse into its medieval past through narrow streets, traditional buildings, and well-preserved city gates.

A Modern Twist on Tradition

While Basel honors its historical roots, the city also embraces modernity and innovation. Its architecture reflects this duality, with new structures designed by renowned architects such as Herzog & de Meuron and Jean Nouvel blending seamlessly with the city's medieval buildings. The city's public spaces, like the Vitra Design Museum and the Tinguely Museum, reflect the city's forward-thinking approach to design and creativity. Basel's architecture exemplifies how a city can remain deeply rooted in its past while constantly evolving and adapting to the present.

Cultural Events and Festivals

Basel is a city that celebrates its cultural identity with events throughout the year. One of the most notable is the Basler Fasnacht, the city's famous carnival. This vibrant festival, featuring colorful parades, music, and elaborate costumes, is a key part of Basel's cultural fabric. Held annually, it draws thousands of visitors who are eager to experience the unique traditions and spirit of the event. The carnival also reflects the city's creative culture, where the arts, community, and history intertwine in a lively display of Basel's cultural energy.

A Hub for Innovation and Technology

Basel's reputation as a center for innovation is evident in its thriving biotechnology and pharmaceutical industries. The city is home to major international companies, including Novartis and Roche, and is a key player in global healthcare and research. This spirit of innovation extends beyond the corporate world and is visible in Basel's support for creative industries, including design and technology. The city hosts events and conferences focused on these fields, making it an ideal destination for those interested in how innovation intersects with culture.

A City by the River

The Rhine River is an essential part of the Basel experience, providing both a natural border and a central feature in the city's daily life. The river offers an opportunity for leisure, with ferries and boats serving as unique modes of transport. The riverbanks are lined with cafés and restaurants, providing spaces for locals and visitors to relax while taking in views of the city. Whether walking along the promenade or enjoying a boat ride, the Rhine adds an element of calm and beauty to the urban landscape, enhancing the overall experience of the city.

Cuisine with a Cultural Fusion

Basel's cuisine reflects the city's multicultural influences, drawing on its Swiss, French, and German heritage. Traditional

Swiss dishes like raclette and fondue can be found alongside French-inspired fare and German specialties. The city is also known for its fine chocolates and local pastries, offering visitors a taste of Basel's culinary craftsmanship. Basel's vibrant food scene is complemented by a growing craft beer industry and a variety of international restaurants that highlight the city's global connections.

Planning Your Trip

Best Time to Visit Basel

Spring (March to May)

Spring is a great time to visit Basel as the city starts to warm up after winter, with temperatures ranging from 10°C to 15°C (50°F to 59°F). This period is also when the Basler Fasnacht (Carnival) takes place, typically in February or March, offering a vibrant and colorful experience. The carnival is one of Switzerland's most famous cultural events, and attending it provides a unique opportunity to see Basel's traditions come to life. The city's parks and outdoor spaces begin to bloom during this time, creating a pleasant atmosphere for sightseeing and exploring.

Summer (June to August)

Summer, from June to August, is Basel's peak tourist season, with temperatures ranging from 20°C to 28°C (68°F to 82°F). This is when the city comes alive with outdoor events, including music festivals, open-air concerts, and cultural activities. The summer weather makes it perfect for enjoying the Rhine River, either by boat or along the banks, where locals and visitors gather to enjoy the warm weather. While it is the busiest season, the vibrant atmosphere and numerous activities make it a popular time for tourists.

Autumn (September to November)

Autumn offers mild temperatures around 10°C to 18°C (50°F to 64°F), making it a comfortable time to visit Basel. The city is less crowded compared to the summer months, allowing for a more relaxed experience. The fall season brings beautiful colors to the surrounding parks and hills, creating scenic views for photographers and nature enthusiasts. The Herbstmesse (Autumn Fair), held in October, is a highlight, offering local food, crafts, and cultural experiences. This period also sees many museums and galleries showcasing new exhibitions, making it an ideal time for cultural exploration.

Winter (December to February)

Winter in Basel is cold, with temperatures ranging from 0°C to 5°C (32°F to 41°F), but it offers a cozy and festive atmosphere. During the Christmas season, Basel's Christmas markets, especially those in the Old Town, are among the best in Switzerland. Visitors can enjoy seasonal treats, handcrafted gifts, and holiday cheer while strolling through beautifully decorated streets. Though the weather can be chilly, indoor attractions like museums and restaurants provide warmth and comfort. Additionally, Basel's proximity to the Swiss Alps makes it convenient for travelers who wish to explore the nearby ski resorts.

Visa Requirements and Entry Information

Schengen Area Visa

Switzerland, including Basel, is part of the Schengen Area, which allows for easier travel between 27 European countries.

If you are from a non-Schengen country, you will need a Schengen visa to enter Switzerland. The visa allows you to travel freely within the Schengen Area for up to 90 days within a 180-day period. Ensure your passport is valid for at least three months beyond your planned departure date. The application process involves providing necessary documents such as proof of accommodation, travel insurance, financial stability, and a flight itinerary.

Visa Exempt Countries

Citizens of certain countries, including the United States, Canada, Australia, and most EU member states, do not require a visa for short stays (up to 90 days) in Switzerland. However, travelers should ensure that their passports are valid for at least three months beyond the date of departure. Entry is typically granted upon arrival, though travelers may need to show proof of sufficient funds, accommodation, and travel plans.

Travel Insurance

Travel insurance is often a requirement for obtaining a Schengen visa. It should cover medical emergencies, repatriation, and any unforeseen circumstances during your stay. Even if not required for visa-free travelers, it is highly recommended to have travel insurance that meets Schengen standards, particularly for health coverage, as medical costs in Switzerland can be high.

Customs and Health Regulations

Switzerland enforces strict customs regulations. You are allowed to bring a limited amount of goods into the country without incurring duties, such as 1 liter of spirits, 200 cigarettes, and 250 grams of tobacco. You should also be aware of Switzerland's health regulations. Travelers may be required to show proof of vaccinations or health certificates, especially if traveling from regions affected by specific diseases, although COVID-19 requirements have eased in most cases.

Arrival Procedures

Upon arrival in Basel, especially if you're entering through the EuroAirport, travelers will go through border control where customs officers may ask for proof of travel plans, accommodation, and sufficient funds. The process is usually efficient, and travelers can proceed to the city quickly. Basel also has direct train connections to Germany and France, and traveling by rail does not involve additional checks when moving between these countries, though you should always carry your passport or ID.

Health and Safety Tips for Travelers

Health Insurance and Emergency Care

It's essential to have travel insurance that covers medical expenses, as healthcare in Switzerland can be expensive. Even if you are not required to show proof of insurance for short stays, it's recommended to have coverage in case of illness or injury. Switzerland has high-quality healthcare facilities, and the emergency number for medical help is 144. If you are traveling from outside the EU, make sure your insurance covers repatriation and emergency treatment, as this can be costly without proper coverage.

Vaccinations and Health Precautions

Before traveling to Basel, it's a good idea to check if you need any vaccinations. For most travelers, routine vaccinations (such as for tetanus, diphtheria, and hepatitis A) are sufficient. If you're traveling from a country with specific health risks, such as yellow fever, you may need proof of vaccination. Switzerland has a clean public health record, and there are generally no specific health risks for tourists. However, it's wise to ensure you're up to date on general vaccinations and carry a health certificate if required.

Drinking Water and Food Safety

Basel has high-quality tap water, and it is safe to drink directly from the tap. There are also many public water fountains throughout the city, especially near parks and public spaces. When it comes to food, Swiss food hygiene standards are high, so eating at restaurants, markets, and food stalls is generally safe. If you have specific dietary restrictions, it's easy to find options, particularly in a cosmopolitan city like Basel, which offers a wide range of international cuisines.

Safety and Security

Basel is generally a safe city with low crime rates, but like any other urban area, you should remain vigilant. Pickpocketing can occasionally be a problem in crowded areas such as tourist attractions or public transport. It's advisable to keep your valuables, including passports, wallets, and electronics, secure and out of sight. Basel also has a well-organized police force, and you can reach them by calling 117 in case of emergencies.

The city's public transport system is safe, but it's always good to be cautious, especially at night.

Weather and Environmental Conditions

Switzerland's weather can be unpredictable, so it's essential to be prepared for changes. In winter, temperatures can drop below freezing, and snowfall is common, especially in the mountainous areas. Be sure to pack warm clothing if you're visiting during this time. In the warmer months, Basel's weather is generally mild, but it can get hot in the summer. Bring sunscreen, wear appropriate clothing, and stay hydrated, especially if you're spending time outdoors or along the Rhine River. Basel is located near the river, so make sure to follow safety rules when swimming or engaging in water activities.

Transportation and Pedestrian Safety

Basel has an excellent public transportation system that includes trams, buses, and trains. It's generally very safe to use, but always be mindful of traffic when crossing streets. Basel has many bike lanes, and cycling is popular, so be cautious if you're walking in areas with heavy bike traffic. Trams are frequent and efficient, but be sure to check schedules or ask locals for guidance when navigating the system. When traveling by taxi, only use official, licensed taxis to ensure safety and fair pricing.

Emergency Services and Local Laws

In case of emergency, you can contact the police by dialing 117, the fire department at 118, and medical emergencies at 144. Basel's emergency services are well-equipped and responsive, and English is widely spoken, so communication is generally not an issue. Switzerland is known for its strict laws, and it's important to be aware of local rules, such as smoking restrictions in public spaces and laws against drug use. Public transportation requires a valid ticket, and fines can be issued for those caught without one.

Currency, Banking, and Local Tips

Currency

Switzerland's official currency is the Swiss Franc (CHF), and it is essential to use CHF for transactions. While some places near the border might accept Euros (EUR), this is not the norm, and the exchange rate may not be favorable. To avoid issues, it's best to use Swiss Francs throughout your stay. You can exchange currency at local banks, exchange offices, or withdraw cash from ATMs. Most places accept credit or debit cards, but it's always good to carry some cash, especially for smaller purchases at markets or local shops.

Banking and ATMs

Basel is well-equipped with ATMs that accept international cards, and you will find these machines at major banks, shopping areas, and transport hubs. Many banks charge a small fee for international card withdrawals, so it's advisable to check with your bank before your trip to avoid unexpected charges. If you need to exchange money, it's usually better to do so at exchange offices in the city, as they offer more favorable rates than those at the airport. Using local ATMs for cash withdrawals is often more cost-effective than exchanging large sums at a time.

Tipping Practices

In Switzerland, tipping is not compulsory, as service charges are often included in restaurant bills. However, tipping is appreciated for good service. In restaurants, rounding up the bill or leaving a 5-10% tip for excellent service is common. For taxis, rounding up to the nearest franc or leaving a few extra francs is customary but not required. In hotels, small tips for bellhops or housekeeping (a few francs) are appreciated. For tour guides or private drivers, a tip of 10-15% is considered polite, especially if the service was exceptional.

Local Etiquette and Behavior

Switzerland values punctuality, so always try to be on time for appointments or events. The Swiss are known for their reserved nature, so it's important to respect personal space, especially in public places. While many people in Basel speak English, particularly in tourist areas, learning a few basic phrases in German, which is the primary language in Basel, can enhance your experience. The Swiss also take cleanliness seriously, so be sure to dispose of waste in the designated bins and keep public spaces clean. Being mindful of local customs and showing respect for personal space will help you blend in smoothly with the local culture.

Public Transport and Travel Tips

Basel offers an excellent public transport system, including trams, buses, and trains, which are reliable and easy to use. The

Basel Card, provided to all overnight guests, offers free travel on public transport within the city, making it convenient for visitors. Always remember to validate your ticket before boarding, as ticket inspectors frequently check for valid tickets. If you plan to explore neighboring regions, such as France or Germany, Basel's location allows easy access to cross-border trains and trams, making day trips to nearby countries simple and straightforward.

Electricity and Plug Types

Switzerland uses the standard European two-pin plug (Type C and Type J) and operates on a 230V supply with a frequency of 50Hz. If your electronic devices have a different plug type or operate on a different voltage, you will need an adapter and possibly a voltage converter. Many hotels and accommodations in Basel provide universal plug sockets, but it's always a good idea to check in advance or bring your own adapter to ensure compatibility with your devices.

Local Language

In Basel, the local language spoken by the majority of residents is Swiss German, specifically the Basel dialect known as Baseldeutsch. This variant of Swiss German is part of the Alemannic dialect group and differs notably from Standard German. The Basel dialect has its own distinct vocabulary, pronunciation, and expressions, which make it unique to the region. While Swiss German is widely used in daily life, the variations in the dialect can make communication with speakers from other parts of Switzerland slightly challenging.

Though Baseldeutsch is common in informal settings, such as conversations with friends or at home, Standard German is the preferred language for formal situations, such as in schools, businesses, and government communications. This is important for visitors, as many written materials and official documentation, including signs and menus in some locations, are in Standard German.

In addition to Swiss German, French is commonly spoken and understood by many residents of Basel, particularly in educational and professional settings. Basel's proximity to the French border makes French an important second language for the region. It is widely taught in schools and often used in cross-border interactions, given that Basel is located at the intersection of Switzerland, Germany, and France. As a result, French speakers will find it relatively easy to communicate in the city, especially in areas such as restaurants, hotels, and shops.

English is also widely spoken in Basel, particularly among younger generations and in business and tourism sectors. Due to Switzerland's high standard of education, many people, especially those working in the service and hospitality industries, have a good command of English. This makes Basel a fairly accessible city for English-speaking travelers, as you can expect most people to understand and respond in English in major tourist areas and public transport.

Emergency Contacts and Important Information

Emergency Numbers

Switzerland has a well-organized emergency response system, and it is important to know the relevant emergency numbers before traveling to Basel. The general emergency number for all services (police, fire, and medical) is 112, which works across Europe. For medical emergencies, you can directly call 144 to reach an ambulance. The police can be contacted by dialing 117, and the fire department can be reached at 118. These numbers are available 24/7, and English is commonly understood by emergency responders, making it easier for non-German or French speakers to communicate.

Local Hospitals and Medical Care

Basel has several high-quality hospitals and healthcare facilities. One of the main hospitals is the University Hospital Basel (Universitätsspital Basel), which provides comprehensive medical care, including emergency services. There are also numerous private clinics and medical centers that offer specialized treatment. Visitors should ensure they have travel insurance that covers medical care, as healthcare in Switzerland can be expensive without proper coverage. For minor injuries or illnesses, local pharmacies (Apotheke) are well-equipped to provide over-the-counter medications and advice.

Pharmacies and Medicines

Pharmacies in Basel are well-distributed across the city, and they often stay open late or offer emergency services. Pharmacies are not only places to buy medications, but also offer medical advice for common ailments. If you require prescription medication, it's a good idea to bring a doctor's note or prescription from your home country, as some medications may require special authorization in Switzerland. The local pharmacies can help you find what you need, and they also provide first aid supplies for minor injuries.

Insurance Requirements

It is highly recommended to have travel insurance that covers health, accidents, and repatriation before visiting Basel. Although Switzerland has a high standard of healthcare, the costs can be significant for visitors without insurance. Ensure your insurance policy covers emergency medical treatment, hospital stays, and any unforeseen incidents. Travel insurance should also cover trip cancellations, lost luggage, or delays. Make sure to keep your insurance policy details and emergency contact numbers with you during your travels.

Police and Lost Property

In case of theft or loss of personal items, the police in Basel can assist you. The police station is easily accessible, and it is always advisable to report any incidents as soon as possible. For lost items, most public transportation stations, hotels, and stores have lost and found services, which help recover lost belongings. If you lose your passport or identification documents, it's crucial to report the loss to the police and the nearest embassy or consulate. Most embassies are located in nearby cities, such as Zurich or Geneva.

Travel Safety

Basel is considered a safe city, with relatively low crime rates. However, as in any urban area, pickpocketing can occur, especially in crowded tourist areas or public transportation. It's essential to be cautious and keep your valuables secure, particularly in busy locations like markets or train stations. Additionally, Basel has a well-maintained public transportation system that is safe and reliable. However, always be aware of your surroundings, especially late at night. When in doubt, use reputable taxi services or official transportation rather than accepting offers from unlicensed drivers.

Legal Considerations

Switzerland has strict laws that should be followed to avoid any legal trouble. Public behavior is expected to be respectful, and there are penalties for things like public drunkenness, smoking in non-designated areas, or disturbing the peace. Drug use is illegal and heavily regulated. It is also important to be aware of local driving laws if you plan to rent a car. For example, driving in Switzerland requires seat belts for all passengers, and speeding fines are hefty. Be mindful of local regulations and follow instructions from authorities to avoid fines or penalties.

Accommodation in Basel

Luxury Hotels

Grand Hotel Les Trois Rois

Address: Blumenrain 8, 4001 Basel, Switzerland Offers: A historic, five-star hotel located along the Rhine River, offering stunning views and luxurious amenities. It features a full-service spa, an upscale restaurant with Michelin-starred dining, and beautifully appointed rooms and suites.

Features: Free Wi-Fi, 24-hour room service, a private dock on the Rhine for river cruises, fitness center, and personalized concierge services.

Estimated Price: CHF 600-1,200 per night, depending on the room and season.

Contact Information: +41 61 260 50 50, info@troisrois.ch

Hotel Krafft Basel

Address: Rheingasse 12, 4058 Basel, Switzerland

Offers: An elegant, historic hotel offering spectacular views of the Rhine and easy access to Basel's cultural sites. It provides modern amenities in a charming, traditional setting.

Features: Restaurant with riverfront dining, free Wi-Fi, a bar, conference rooms, and proximity to key attractions like the Kunstmuseum.

Estimated Price: CHF 300-600 per night.

Contact Information: +41 61 690 60 00, info@krafft-basel.ch

The Passage

Address: Steinentorstrasse 10, 4051 Basel, Switzerland

Offers: A stylish and modern boutique hotel in the heart of Basel. It offers an excellent blend of luxury and design with a wellness area, restaurant, and an elegant bar.

Features: Free Wi-Fi, fitness center, rooftop terrace, spa services, and pet-friendly accommodations.

Estimated Price: CHF 250-500 per night.

Contact Information: +41 61 225 99 99, info@the-passage.ch

Hotel Basel

Address: Mäckerngasse 4, 4001 Basel, Switzerland

Offers: A luxurious four-star hotel in Basel's Old Town, offering modern rooms with historical charm. The hotel is known for its personalized service and proximity to museums and cultural centers.

Features: Free Wi-Fi, restaurant and bar, rooftop terrace with panoramic views, and fitness center.

Estimated Price: CHF 250-450 per night.

Contact Information: +41 61 560 88 88, info@hotelbasel.ch

Mid-Range Hotels

Hotel Spalentor Basel

Address: Spalenberg 10, 4051 Basel, Switzerland

Offers: A charming, mid-range hotel located near the Old Town, offering a mix of modern design and comfort. Ideal for both business and leisure travelers.

Features: Free Wi-Fi, buffet breakfast, fitness center, bike rental, and pet-friendly rooms.

Estimated Price: CHF 150-250 per night.

Contact Information: +41 61 690 10 00, info@spalentor.ch

Hotel Bildungszentrum 21

Address: Klosterstrasse 21, 4057 Basel, Switzerland

Offers: A comfortable and affordable option with modern rooms and a peaceful atmosphere, perfect for those visiting Basel for business or leisure.

Features: Free Wi-Fi, on-site restaurant with a garden, conference facilities, and fitness center.

Estimated Price: CHF 150-220 per night.

Contact Information: +41 61 315 11 11, info@hotel21.ch

Hotel Gasthof zum. Neuen Markt

Address: Neuweilerstrasse 15, 4052 Basel, Switzerland

Offers: A well-maintained hotel with a traditional Swiss feel. The hotel's location allows easy access to the Old Town and public transport.

Features: Free Wi-Fi, restaurant, parking, and breakfast service.

Estimated Price: CHF 120-220 per night.

Contact Information: +41 61 271 16 61, info@zum-neuen-markt.ch

Hotel Victoria

Address: Centralbahnplatz 3-4, 4002 Basel, Switzerland

Offers: A mid-range hotel situated conveniently near the Basel train station and city center. A comfortable base for tourists looking to explore Basel's landmarks.

Features: Free Wi-Fi, restaurant, conference rooms, pet-friendly, and fitness center.

Estimated Price: CHF 150-250 per night.

Contact Information: +41 61 685 50 50, info@hotelvictoria.ch

Budget Hotels

EasyHotel Basel

Address: Riehenring 109, 4058 Basel, Switzerland

Offers: A budget-friendly, no-frills hotel with clean, simple rooms in a convenient location. It's ideal for travelers looking for an affordable stay with easy access to public transport and the city center.

Features: Free Wi-Fi, 24-hour reception, and basic amenities.

Estimated Price: CHF 80-150 per night.

Contact Information: +41 61 561 97 97, basel@easyhotel.com

Hotel Restaurant Eremitage

Address: Hochbergerstrasse 60, 4057 Basel, Switzerland

Offers: A reasonably priced hotel that combines comfort and practicality. It is located slightly outside the city center but well-connected by public transport.

Features: Free Wi-Fi, restaurant, free parking, and breakfast options.

Estimated Price: CHF 100-180 per night.

Contact Information: +41 61 319 35 35, info@eremitage.ch

Basel Backpack

Address: Hochstrasse 57, 4053 Basel, Switzerland

Offers: A budget hostel option for travelers looking for a communal, casual experience. Located close to Basel's public transport, it's great for backpackers and budget-conscious travelers.

Features: Free Wi-Fi, dormitory rooms, a shared kitchen, and a lounge area.

Estimated Price: CHF 30-80 per night.

Contact Information: +41 61 511 34 80, info@baselbackpack.ch

Hotel Restaurant Kloster Dornach

Address: Dornacherstrasse 9, 4143 Dornach, Switzerland

Offers: A budget-friendly hotel located a little outside Basel in Dornach, ideal for travelers looking for a quiet retreat.

Features: Free Wi-Fi, restaurant, and complimentary parking.

Estimated Price: CHF 90-150 per night.Contact Information: +41 61 705 47 47, info@kloster-dornach.ch

Other Accommodation Categories

Airbnb and Short-Term Rentals

Basel offers a variety of short-term rental options through platforms like Airbnb, catering to those who prefer a more personalized or homely experience. Whether you're looking for a private apartment, a shared room, or a house, there are many options available across different price ranges. Rentals are popular for longer stays or those looking for more flexibility. Prices vary significantly depending on location and size, ranging from CHF 80 to CHF 500 per night.

Hostels and Guesthouses

Basel has several hostels and guesthouses that provide affordable accommodation for younger travelers or those on a budget. These places often feature communal kitchens, shared rooms, and a social atmosphere. Hostel options like "Basel Backpack" and "Youth Hostel Basel" are ideal for budget-conscious travelers. Expect prices from CHF 40 to CHF 80 per night.

Serviced Apartments

For those staying in Basel for extended periods or requiring self-catering options, serviced apartments offer a balance of comfort and convenience. Properties like "Adagio Basel City" provide fully equipped kitchens and home-like amenities, ideal for longer stays. Prices vary, typically ranging from CHF 150 to CHF 250 per night, depending on the apartment size and location.

Getting to and Around Basel

Getting to Basel

By Air (EuroAirport Basel-Mulhouse-Freiburg)

Basel is served by EuroAirport Basel-Mulhouse-Freiburg (BSL/MLH/EAP), located just 6 kilometers (3.7 miles) from the city center. This airport is a hub for both domestic and international flights, with connections to major cities across Europe and beyond. The airport serves as a convenient entry point for tourists flying into Basel. Upon arrival, you can take a taxi or the number 50 bus, which connects the airport to Basel SBB (Basel's main train station) in about 20 minutes. Taxis will cost around CHF 30-40 to get to the city center, while the bus is a more economical option, at around CHF 3-5 for a one-way ticket.

By Train

Basel is well-connected to other European cities by train. The city's main station, Basel SBB, is one of Switzerland's busiest, offering direct connections to major cities like Zurich, Geneva, Paris, and Frankfurt. The high-speed trains, such as the TGV and ICE, provide quick and comfortable travel. Basel's central location makes it an ideal base for exploring neighboring countries, and you can reach other Swiss cities or cities in France and Germany within a couple of hours. The station is easily accessible from all areas of Basel, and taxis or buses can take you from the station to your accommodation in just a few minutes.

By Car

If you're planning to rent a car, Basel is easily accessible by road. The city is well-connected to major highways, and you can drive in from neighboring countries such as France and Germany. Keep in mind that Switzerland requires a highway vignette (toll sticker) to drive on motorways, which can be purchased at gas stations or border crossings. Parking in Basel can be challenging, particularly in the city center, so it's advisable to book accommodations with parking facilities or use one of the many public parking garages available throughout the city.

By Bus

Basel is also reachable by long-distance bus services, such as FlixBus, which connect the city to other European destinations. While this option is more budget-friendly, bus journeys tend to take longer than train or air travel. Buses generally arrive and depart from the Basel central bus station, which is located near the main train station.

Getting Around Basel

Public Transport

Basel has an excellent public transportation system that is easy to navigate. The Basel tram network is extensive, with trams running frequently throughout the day. Trams are the most popular and convenient way to get around, with routes covering most of the city and surrounding areas. The city's bus system also complements the tram network, providing access to areas not covered by trams. Tickets for trams and buses can be purchased at ticket machines or via mobile apps, and they are valid for both modes of transport. The Basel Card, given to overnight guests of the city, offers unlimited travel on public transportation, making it a convenient option for tourists. For those staying in Basel, public transport is not only efficient but also environmentally friendly.

Biking

Basel is a bike-friendly city with an extensive network of bike lanes and cycling routes. Many visitors choose to rent bikes to explore the city at their own pace. The city has several bike rental services, and some accommodations provide bikes for guests. Basel's proximity to the Rhine River also makes cycling along the river a scenic and enjoyable experience. The city has a bike-sharing system called "BSV," where you can rent a bike for short trips. Biking is a great way to explore Basel's parks, the Old Town, and the riverbanks while enjoying the fresh air and avoiding traffic.

Walking

Basel is a compact city with many attractions located close to each other, making walking one of the best ways to explore. The Old Town, with its cobbled streets, is pedestrian-friendly and offers many historical sites, museums, cafes, and shops within walking distance. Walking along the Rhine River, visiting the numerous fountains, or exploring the lively Marktplatz are all great ways to experience the city's atmosphere. Since the city is walkable and well-maintained, it's easy to explore on foot without worrying about getting lost.

Taxis and Ride-Sharing

Taxis are available throughout Basel, but they tend to be more expensive compared to public transportation or biking. Taxis can be hailed on the street or booked by phone. Uber operates in Basel, providing an alternative to traditional taxis. Ride-sharing services like Uber are a convenient option for those who prefer door-to-door service without the need for public transport. While more expensive than buses or trams, they are a good option when traveling with luggage or in a group.

River Ferries

One of Basel's unique and charming modes of transportation is its river ferry service. The Basel ferries, which are powered solely by the current of the Rhine River, provide a fun and scenic way to cross the river. There are several ferry routes that connect the city's two banks, with ferries operating from early morning to late evening. This is a popular mode of transport for locals and tourists alike, especially during warmer months. The ferries are free for those holding a Basel Card, making it an attractive option for tourists

Car Rentals and Parking

Although Basel is a city well-served by public transport, some visitors may prefer to rent a car for day trips outside the city or to explore the surrounding regions of Switzerland, France, and

Germany. Car rental services are available at EuroAirport and throughout the city. However, parking in Basel can be limited and expensive, particularly in the city center. It is advisable to use public transport or park in one of the many parking garages on the outskirts of the city to avoid the hassle of finding parking in the busy areas.

Insider Tips and Recommendations

Public Transport Tickets

If you're planning to use public transport frequently during your stay, consider purchasing a Basel Card, which offers unlimited travel on the city's trams, buses, and trains. The card also includes discounts on various attractions and is often given to hotel guests as part of their accommodation.

Walking Tours

If you prefer a guided experience, consider joining a walking tour. There are many tours available that cover the city's history, culture, and landmarks, and they provide valuable insights into Basel's past and present. Walking tours allow you to experience the city from a local perspective and are often led by knowledgeable guides who can offer insider tips and recommendations.

Cycling on the Rhine

Basel's riverside paths are a popular destination for cyclists, and riding along the Rhine offers great views of the city. Whether you rent a bike for a few hours or use a bike-sharing service, cycling along the river is a pleasant and scenic way to explore Basel at a relaxed pace. Make sure to take advantage of the city's bike lanes and paths, which make cycling both safe and enjoyable.

Use the Basel Card for Discounts

The Basel Card not only offers unlimited public transport access but also provides discounts to many of the city's top attractions, including museums, galleries, and tours. It can be an excellent investment for visitors planning to explore the city's cultural offerings.

Museums and Galleries

Overview of Basel's Vibrant Art Scene

Kunstmuseum Basel

The Kunstmuseum Basel is Switzerland's oldest public art collection, founded in 1661. Located in the heart of the city, this museum houses an impressive collection of works spanning centuries, including pieces by Renaissance masters, modern artists like van Gogh, Cézanne, and Picasso, as well as contemporary art. The museum offers a comprehensive look at the evolution of European art, making it a must-visit for anyone interested in art history. In addition to its permanent collection, the Kunstmuseum regularly hosts temporary exhibitions that bring new artists and themes to the forefront. The museum's central location makes it easily accessible, and it provides insight into Basel's historical role as a cultural hub.

Art Basel Fair

Art Basel is one of the most prestigious and influential contemporary art fairs in the world. Held annually in Basel, this event brings together artists, collectors, and galleries from around the globe to showcase cutting-edge contemporary art in a variety of media, from painting and sculpture to digital art and performance. Art Basel not only highlights established artists but also provides a platform for emerging talents. The fair attracts thousands of art enthusiasts each year and has become a key part of Basel's identity as a center for contemporary art. For visitors, the fair is an opportunity to engage with the global art scene and experience the latest trends in the art world.

Fondation Beyeler

Located just outside the city in Riehen, the Fondation Beyeler is a private museum that showcases an exceptional collection of modern classics. With works by artists like Monet, Picasso, van Gogh, and Rousseau, the museum provides a comprehensive overview of modern art movements. The museum itself is a work of art, designed by architect Renzo Piano to blend seamlessly with the surrounding landscape. The Fondation Beyeler is known for its tranquil atmosphere, making it an ideal place for reflection and inspiration. Its surrounding gardens, which display sculptures, also offer visitors a unique outdoor experience that complements the art inside.

Tinguely Museum

Dedicated to the work of Swiss artist Jean Tinguely, the Tinguely Museum is a must-see for those interested in kinetic and mechanical art. Located near the Rhine River, the museum features many of Tinguely's large-scale, moving sculptures, as well as his drawings and models. The museum offers visitors a glimpse into the artist's playful and experimental approach to art, combining humor, technology, and social commentary. The Tinguely Museum not only showcases the work of one of

Basel's most famous artists but also hosts temporary exhibitions by other contemporary artists, expanding its influence beyond the work of Tinguely himself.

Public Art and Street Art

Basel's art scene extends beyond museums and galleries into the streets. The city is home to a growing collection of public art installations, murals, and sculptures that are integrated into its public spaces. This includes works by international street artists as well as local artists, offering visitors a chance to experience art in a more casual and accessible setting. Basel's commitment to public art reflects its desire to make art a part of everyday life, engaging residents and visitors alike. Walking through Basel, you will encounter a wide variety of art, from temporary street art projects to permanent sculptures and installations that reflect the city's contemporary art culture.

Basel's Cultural Institutions

In addition to its renowned museums, Basel is home to numerous cultural institutions that contribute to the city's vibrant art scene. The Kunsthalle Basel is one of the leading contemporary art spaces, regularly showcasing new artists and experimental exhibitions. The city also has a number of smaller galleries and independent art spaces that focus on emerging artists, alternative art forms, and cutting-edge practices. Basel's commitment to art education, with institutions like the Hochschule für Gestaltung und Kunst (University of Art and Design), also ensures that the city remains at the forefront of creative innovation.

Must-Visit Museums and Galleries

Kunstmuseum Basel

The Kunstmuseum Basel is one of Switzerland's oldest and most important public art collections, offering a comprehensive range of art spanning from the Renaissance to contemporary works. Located in the city center, it features an extensive collection of European art, including pieces from artists like van Gogh, Cézanne, Picasso, and more. The museum regularly holds temporary exhibitions and offers educational programs, making it a must-visit for art enthusiasts. With its convenient location and wide-ranging collections, it is one of Basel's top cultural attractions.

Fondation Beyeler

Located just outside Basel in Riehen, the Fondation Beyeler is a private museum known for its collection of modern and contemporary art. It includes works by iconic artists such as Monet, van Gogh, Picasso, and Rousseau. The museum's modern architecture, designed by Renzo Piano, is complemented by its beautiful gardens where visitors can view sculptures and art installations. The museum regularly hosts temporary exhibitions, further enhancing its role as a key player in Basel's art scene. It's an ideal place for those who appreciate a combination of art and nature.

Tinguely Museum

Dedicated to the works of Swiss artist Jean Tinguely, the Tinguely Museum offers a unique collection of kinetic and mechanical art. Located near the Rhine River, the museum showcases Tinguely's large-scale sculptures that move and interact, providing an interactive experience for visitors. Along with permanent exhibitions, the museum hosts temporary shows by contemporary artists that explore similar themes of motion and technology. It is an essential stop for anyone interested in innovative and experimental art.

Kunsthalle Basel

Kunsthalle Basel is one of the most important contemporary art spaces in Switzerland. Known for its innovative exhibitions and support of emerging artists, the gallery regularly hosts experimental and avant-garde exhibitions. Located in the heart of Basel, Kunsthalle offers a dynamic program that challenges traditional notions of art and its boundaries. It is a popular spot for art lovers looking to explore the latest trends and ideas in the contemporary art world.

Vitra Design Museum

Situated just outside Basel in the nearby town of Weil am Rhein, the Vitra Design Museum is a leading institution for design, architecture, and applied arts. The museum showcases design collections ranging from furniture design to architecture, with works by notable designers like Charles and Ray Eames, Frank Gehry, and Zaha Hadid. The museum also offers a variety of special exhibitions and is known for its impressive building, designed by Frank Gehry. It is a must-visit for those interested in design and architecture.

Museum Tinguely

Another museum dedicated to Jean Tinguely, this institution offers a deep dive into the artist's life and work. The museum showcases his innovative kinetic art and is housed in a striking building designed by the architect Mario Botta. The museum's permanent collection features many of Tinguely's mechanical sculptures, offering a unique insight into his artistic process. It's an excellent spot for visitors interested in interactive and experimental art.

Museum der Kulturen

The Museum der Kulturen (Museum of Cultures) focuses on anthropology and world cultures, with collections from Africa, Asia, the Americas, and Oceania. It provides an in-depth look at cultural history, exploring various global traditions, rituals, and artifacts. This museum also highlights the relationship between different cultures and offers exhibitions on contemporary issues like migration and identity. It's a great destination for those interested in learning about global cultures and history.

Specialized Art Spaces and Exhibitions

Kunsthalle Basel

Kunsthalle Basel is one of the leading spaces for contemporary art in Switzerland. Located in the heart of the city, it is known for its progressive approach to art exhibitions, often showcasing experimental and avant-garde works. Kunsthalle's program is dynamic, with rotating exhibitions that often feature emerging artists or tackle current social issues. It is a space where new ideas and concepts are regularly explored, making it a key institution in Basel's art scene. Visitors can expect exhibitions that challenge conventional notions of art, providing a platform for thought-provoking dialogue.

Vitra Design Museum

Although technically just outside Basel in Weil am Rhein, the Vitra Design Museum is an essential part of Basel's design culture. This museum focuses on the intersection of design, architecture, and art, offering exhibitions that explore modern and contemporary design history. It is home to the world's most important design collections, including works from iconic designers such as Charles and Ray Eames and Frank Gehry. The museum's architecture, designed by Frank Gehry, adds another layer of interest, combining cutting-edge design with thought-provoking exhibitions that explore how design shapes our lives.

Fondation Beyeler

Located in the nearby suburb of Riehen, the Fondation Beyeler is not only a museum but also an essential part of Basel's specialized art space landscape. The museum focuses on modern and contemporary art and is housed in a purpose-built building designed by Renzo Piano. It is known for its carefully curated collection, which includes works from artists like Monet, Cézanne, van Gogh, and Picasso. The exhibitions at Fondation Beyeler often have a thematic focus, offering visitors an in-depth look at different art movements and the artists who shaped them. The museum's serene environment and beautifully landscaped gardens complement its collections, making it an ideal space for reflection and artistic appreciation.

The Tinguely Museum

The Tinguely Museum is dedicated to the works of Jean Tinguely, a Swiss artist known for his kinetic art and mechanical sculptures. The museum showcases his large-scale works that incorporate movement and sound, offering an interactive experience for visitors. It also hosts temporary exhibitions that explore themes of movement, technology, and the interaction between art and science. As one of the most specialized museums in Basel, it offers a unique look at an artist who redefined art by incorporating machines and movement into his creations.

Haus der Elektronischen Künste

The Haus der Elektronischen Künste is Basel's premier space for electronic and digital arts. Located in the city center, it showcases works that explore the intersection of technology, art, and innovation. The exhibitions at Haus der Elektronischen

Künste focus on new media, digital art, virtual reality, and sound art, providing visitors with an understanding of how technology influences contemporary art. The museum offers a space for artists working with new forms of media to present their work, often integrating interactive elements that engage visitors in the creative process.

Museum für Gegenwartskunst

The Museum für Gegenwartskunst (Museum of Contemporary Art) in Basel is another vital art space dedicated to presenting cutting-edge art. This museum is known for its rotating exhibitions of contemporary artists and experimental installations. It provides a platform for both established and emerging artists to showcase their work, and its exhibitions often address themes of identity, politics, and culture. The museum's focus on contemporary art makes it a key location for anyone interested in the latest developments in the art world.

Exploring Contemporary Art in Basel

Art Basel

Art Basel is one of the world's most prestigious contemporary art fairs, held annually in Basel. It attracts artists, galleries, collectors, and curators from across the globe, making it a central event for anyone involved in the contemporary art world. The fair showcases a wide range of media, including paintings, sculptures, video installations, and performances. Art Basel provides a platform for both well-established and emerging artists, offering a comprehensive overview of current trends in contemporary art. For visitors, it's an opportunity to view cutting-edge works and engage with the global art community.

Kunsthalle Basel

Kunsthalle Basel, one of Switzerland's foremost institutions for contemporary art, is known for its experimental exhibitions and innovative approach to curating. The gallery frequently hosts exhibitions that push boundaries and present art that questions societal norms and explores complex contemporary issues. The focus is often on emerging artists, offering them a space to present new works. Kunsthalle Basel's program encourages diverse artistic practices and aims to challenge conventional ideas, making it an essential stop for visitors interested in the evolution of contemporary art.

Museum für Gegenwartskunst

The Museum für Gegenwartskunst (Museum of Contemporary Art) in Basel is a key venue for those interested in modern artistic expressions. The museum regularly hosts exhibitions that address current social, political, and environmental concerns, often providing a critical look at global issues through the lens of contemporary art. It also offers a platform for both established and new artists, showcasing works that encourage dialogue and reflection. The museum's forward-thinking exhibitions ensure its place as a key part of Basel's contemporary art scene.

Haus der Elektronischen Künste

Basel's Haus der Elektronischen Künste focuses on the intersection of contemporary art and digital technologies. The museum explores new media, virtual reality, sound art, and interactive installations, providing a space for technology-driven art forms. It regularly presents exhibitions that examine how advancements in technology are reshaping the way art is produced and experienced. This institution is crucial for visitors interested in the role of technology in contemporary artistic practices, highlighting innovative and interactive art forms that engage with both the artist and the audience in new ways.

Tinguely Museum

While primarily dedicated to the works of Jean Tinguely, the Tinguely Museum also explores the broader realm of kinetic art, which continues to influence contemporary artists. The museum showcases Tinguely's mechanical sculptures and interactive installations, offering a dynamic perspective on the relationship between art, technology, and movement. The museum hosts temporary exhibitions that connect Tinguely's work to modern-day practices, offering a fresh take on how movement and technology continue to shape the contemporary art landscape. The museum's unique focus on kinetic art provides an interesting viewpoint for those looking to understand the intersections between contemporary art and mechanical engineering.

Fondation Beyeler

Fondation Beyeler, located just outside Basel in Riehen, presents a curated selection of modern and contemporary art. While it is best known for its collection of 20th-century masters like Monet, Picasso, and Cézanne, the museum also hosts important contemporary art exhibitions. These exhibitions often focus on global themes and the ongoing dialogue between art and society. With its serene setting and beautiful grounds, the museum provides a tranquil environment in which to explore contemporary works that reflect current social, environmental, and cultural issues.

Shopping in Basel

Shopping Guide for Basel

Kaufhaus Basel

Kaufhaus Basel is one of the most iconic department stores in the city, located on the main shopping street, Freie Strasse. This store offers a wide selection of fashion, accessories, beauty products, and home goods. It's a good place to find Swiss brands and European designer labels. Whether you're looking for high-end clothing or unique Swiss souvenirs, Kaufhaus Basel provides a broad range of options. The store's location on Freie Strasse, which is one of Basel's most famous shopping streets, makes it easily accessible.

Estimated Price: Clothing from CHF 50-300, beauty products from CHF 30-100, accessories from CHF 40-200.

Freie Strasse

Freie Strasse is Basel's main shopping street and offers everything from high-end international brands to local boutiques. Walking along this street, you'll find a variety of stores offering clothing, shoes, watches, and jewelry. Basel is known for its watchmaking industry, so this street is ideal for purchasing Swiss watches. The street also has several art galleries and souvenir shops. For fashion, you can find stores like Zara, H&M, and Swiss luxury brands like Bally.

Insider Tip: If you're looking for Swiss-made watches, stores like Bucherer and Swatch are located along Freie Strasse and offer a wide selection. Swiss watches typically start around CHF 100 for entry-level models, while luxury brands can go up to CHF 10,000 and beyond.

Basel's Old Town

Basel's Old Town is a great place to shop for unique items and souvenirs. The narrow cobblestone streets are lined with independent shops selling everything from handmade Swiss chocolates and artisanal cheeses to locally crafted jewelry and Swiss-made watches. For a taste of local culture, stop by one of the many artisan shops offering hand-blown glassware, wooden toys, and Swiss folk art. The Old Town also features several small bookstores offering books on Basel's history, art, and culture.

Estimated Price: Local chocolates from CHF 10-30, handmade jewelry from CHF 30-200, artisanal crafts from CHF 15-100.

Marktplatz

Marktplatz, located in the heart of Basel's Old Town, is home to the city's famous daily market. While the market primarily offers fresh produce, local delicacies, and flowers, it's also a fantastic place to shop for unique Swiss products. You'll find locally-made honey, fresh herbs, artisanal soaps, and small gifts. It's an ideal place for tourists looking to purchase authentic Basel souvenirs.

Insider Tip: For authentic Swiss food souvenirs, the local cheese stands at Marktplatz offer some of the best Swiss cheeses, like Emmental or Gruyère. Prices for cheese can range from CHF 15-30 per kg.

Markthalle Basel

Markthalle Basel is a large, indoor market offering a wide range of food, drinks, and specialty products. Located near the train station, it's a great spot to pick up gourmet products, including local chocolates, Swiss wines, and deli items. Many of the stalls sell handcrafted products like jams, spreads, and specialty teas. If you're looking for Swiss gourmet souvenirs, this market is the place to go.

Estimated Price: Swiss chocolate from CHF 10-30, gourmet jams and spreads from CHF 8-20, local wines from CHF 15-50.

St. Jakob-Park Shopping Mall

St. Jakob-Park is Basel's largest shopping center and offers a wide range of stores under one roof. This mall is ideal for those looking for a more traditional shopping experience, featuring international and Swiss brands like Mango, Nike, and H&M. There is also a selection of home goods stores, electronics, and even a supermarket.

Insider Tip: For fashion-forward shoppers, St. Jakob-Park is home to several sportswear stores, ideal for finding outdoor gear or activewear. Prices for clothing and accessories range from CHF 40 to CHF 150, depending on the brand.

Basel's Watch Shops

Basel is known worldwide for its watchmaking industry, and shopping for Swiss watches is a must for many visitors. If you're interested in purchasing a Swiss watch, consider visiting the local watch shops like Bucherer, which carries luxury Swiss brands such as Rolex, Omega, and Patek Philippe. The prices for Swiss watches can vary significantly based on the brand, model, and features. Entry-level Swiss watches start around CHF 100-500, while luxury models can range from CHF 2,000 to over CHF 50,000 for exclusive pieces.

Insider Tip: If you're looking for a great deal, visit watch shops during the Baselworld trade show (held annually in March), where special offers and exclusive models are often available.

Basel's Christmas Markets (Seasonal)

If you're visiting Basel during the holiday season, don't miss out on the Christmas markets. Basel's Christmas markets, particularly the ones located around the Münster and in the Old Town, offer a range of unique holiday-themed items, including handcrafted ornaments, decorations, and seasonal food. You'll find local Swiss crafts, woodwork, and festive sweets like Swiss gingerbread cookies. Estimated Price: Holiday ornaments from CHF 10-30, handmade gifts from CHF 20-50.

Hidden Gems in Basel

Secret Courtyards and Alleys

Tinguely Fountain Courtyard

Hidden near the Tinguely Museum, the Tinguely Fountain Courtyard is a peaceful spot where visitors can enjoy quiet moments away from the hustle and bustle of Basel. This small courtyard is home to a fountain designed by artist Jean Tinguely, and it offers a tranquil atmosphere perfect for relaxing or taking in some local art. The location is often overlooked by tourists, making it a hidden gem for those seeking a quiet retreat in the city. The courtyard's surroundings include lovely greenery and views of the museum's architecture, enhancing the experience of the space.

Basel's Old Town Alleys

Basel's Old Town is known for its narrow, winding alleys that are steeped in history. These charming passageways, such as the St. Johanns-Vorstadt and the lane leading to the Basel

Minster, are often overlooked by tourists but offer a glimpse into the city's past. Many of these alleys are lined with traditional Swiss houses, boutique shops, and cafes, offering an authentic and quiet exploration of the city. Exploring these alleys provides an opportunity to step back in time, as the cobblestones and historical architecture reflect Basel's medieval charm.

The Münster Hinterhof (Courtyard Behind Basel Minster)

The Münster Hinterhof is a lesser-known courtyard located behind the Basel Minster, providing visitors with a secluded space to admire the church's impressive architecture. The courtyard offers a stunning view of the Rhine River and the city, away from the more crowded areas of the Minster. This peaceful spot is perfect for those wanting to escape the busy tourist routes and take in the beauty of Basel in a more intimate setting. The courtyard is accessible through a hidden path that leads away from the main entrance of the Minster, offering a more serene experience.

The Old City Gate (Stadtmauer and Courtyard)

Located near the St. Alban district, the Old City Gate is one of Basel's most historically significant sites. The gate is part of the medieval city walls and is surrounded by a small courtyard that offers a glimpse into Basel's ancient defenses. Visitors who wander through this area can enjoy the quiet atmosphere and appreciate the preserved elements of the city's past. The surrounding area also includes several old buildings, making it an ideal place for a leisurely walk through Basel's history.

Klingental Quarter and Courtyards

The Klingental Quarter is an area of Basel that is often missed by tourists but offers a variety of beautiful hidden courtyards. This district is home to some of the city's oldest buildings, and the courtyards within this area offer a peaceful escape from the more heavily trafficked parts of Basel. Many of the courtyards feature traditional Swiss architecture, with blooming flowers and benches, providing a picturesque setting. Visitors can explore the narrow paths that lead into these hidden spaces and discover a quiet, less commercialized side of Basel.

Lesser-Known Museums and Art Spaces

Museum der Kulturen

Located in Basel's Old Town, the Museum der Kulturen (Museum of Cultures) is an anthropology museum that offers a unique look at world cultures. While not as widely known as some of Basel's larger institutions, it boasts an impressive collection of artifacts from Africa, Asia, the Americas, and Oceania. The museum's exhibits explore various aspects of human culture, from traditional rituals to contemporary global issues such as migration and identity. For visitors interested in cultural history, this museum provides a lesser-known but fascinating perspective on the world's diverse societies.

Estimated Price: CHF 10-15 for adult entry.

Vitra Design Museum

Although technically located in Weil am Rhein, just outside Basel, the Vitra Design Museum is an essential stop for design enthusiasts. It focuses on the history of design and architecture, housing collections that range from iconic pieces of furniture design to architecture exhibitions by renowned designers such as Frank Gehry and Zaha Hadid. While it may not be as famous as other Basel museums, the Vitra Design Museum is an excellent resource for those interested in the intersection of art and design.

Estimated Price: CHF 15-20 for adult entry.

Pharmacy Museum of the University of Basel

The Pharmacy Museum, located within the University of Basel, offers a deep dive into the history of medicine and pharmaceuticals. It's a hidden gem for visitors interested in the development of medical practices and the science of pharmacy.

The museum showcases an extensive collection of apothecary tools, old medicines, and historical documents related to the evolution of pharmacology. With many unique exhibits, it offers an educational and less commercialized alternative to the larger museums in Basel.

Estimated Price: CHF 8-12 for adult entry.

Antikenmuseum Basel

The Antikenmuseum Basel is a small but significant museum dedicated to ancient civilizations. It houses an impressive collection of artifacts from ancient Greece, Egypt, Rome, and the Near East. The museum's focus on antiquities makes it a perfect stop for those interested in classical history and archaeology. While not as crowded as other museums in Basel, its exhibitions provide detailed insights into the cultural and artistic achievements of ancient civilizations.

Estimated Price: CHF 10-15 for adult entry.

Kunsthalle Basel's Project Space

Kunsthalle Basel is well-known for its main exhibitions, but it also has a lesser-known project space that focuses on experimental and emerging art. This space is used to present works by newer artists who are pushing the boundaries of contemporary art. Exhibitions here often address social, political, and environmental issues through various media, including video, installations, and performances. The project space offers a more intimate experience, where visitors can explore thought-provoking works before they gain wider recognition.

Estimated Price: CHF 5-10 for entry to project space.

Tinguely Museum's Temporary Exhibitions

While the Tinguely Museum is famous for its permanent collection of kinetic art, it also hosts a variety of temporary exhibitions by contemporary artists. These exhibitions often explore themes related to movement, technology, and the interaction between art and mechanics, similar to Tinguely's own work. For visitors who have already explored the main collection, these temporary exhibitions provide a fresh perspective on contemporary art in Basel.

Estimated Price: CHF 15-20 for adult entry, with temporary exhibition prices varying.

Basel Paper Mill Museum

The Basel Paper Mill Museum (Papiermühle) is an often-overlooked museum that provides insight into the history of paper production. Located along the banks of the Rhine, the museum is housed in a historic building that dates back to the 15th century. It offers visitors the opportunity to learn about the traditional methods of papermaking and includes hands-on workshops where you can create your own paper. This museum is ideal for those interested in industrial history or the process behind a vital part of daily life.

Estimated Price: CHF 8-12 for adult entry.

Unusual Spots for Art and History Enthusiasts

Basel Paper Mill Museum

The Basel Paper Mill Museum offers a unique historical perspective on paper production and its role in communication and commerce. Housed in a 15th-century building along the Rhine, this museum provides an immersive experience where visitors can observe the old methods of papermaking. You can even try your hand at making your own paper in workshops. For art and history enthusiasts, the museum provides an intriguing connection between traditional craftsmanship and modern publishing, making it an unusual but insightful stop in Basel.

Estimated Price: CHF 8-12 for adult entry.

Basel's City Walls and Gates

While not a traditional museum, Basel's medieval city walls and gates provide a fascinating look into the city's defensive history. Parts of the ancient city wall, including the St. Johanns Tor and the Spalentor, are still intact and accessible. These structures, built during the Middle Ages, tell the story of Basel's growth and strategic importance. History enthusiasts can walk along the remnants of the city wall, offering a rare opportunity to step into Basel's past and gain a new perspective on the city's history beyond its museums.

Estimated Price: Free, though guided tours may be available for a fee.

Tinguely Fountain Courtyard

Hidden near the Tinguely Museum, the Tinguely Fountain Courtyard is a lesser-known spot that combines art with an element of playfulness. This courtyard, featuring Jean Tinguely's kinetic sculptures, provides a quiet, interactive experience away from the more crowded attractions. The fountain's sculptures move in response to the surrounding elements, adding an unexpected dimension to your visit. Art enthusiasts will appreciate how this space blends public art with the environment, providing a dynamic, but serene, artistic experience.

Estimated Price: Free.

Basel's Hidden Courtyards in the Old Town

Basel's Old Town is full of narrow streets, charming alleys, and hidden courtyards that offer a quiet escape from the main tourist areas. Some of these courtyards are tucked behind buildings and feature traditional Swiss architecture, colorful flowers, and occasional sculptures or art installations. These spots are perfect for art and history lovers who wish to discover hidden gems. Exploring these secret corners of Basel will reveal the city's lesser-known historical and architectural elements, providing a more personal and intimate experience of the city's past.Estimated Price: Free.

Basel's Hidden Museums and Art Spaces

While Basel is home to well-known museums, it also has a range of smaller, lesser-visited museums that focus on specific areas of art and history. The **Pharmacy Museum** at the University of Basel, for example, offers a look into the history of medicine and pharmaceuticals. Similarly, the **Antikenmuseum Basel** offers a specialized collection of artifacts from ancient civilizations. These hidden spots often focus on niche areas of art and history, providing a rich, focused experience for those looking to explore Basel's cultural landscape in more depth.

Estimated Price: CHF 8-15 for adult entry.

Kunsthalle Basel's Project Space

In addition to its main exhibitions, Kunsthalle Basel offers a unique project space for experimental and contemporary art. This lesser-known part of the institution is dedicated to new media and experimental works that may not fit into traditional exhibition formats. It's an intriguing spot for art enthusiasts looking for cutting-edge or thought-provoking exhibitions. The space often features artists who tackle social, political, or environmental issues through innovative mediums, providing visitors with a fresh take on contemporary art. Estimated Price: CHF 5-10 for entry to the project space.

Klingental Quarter

The Klingental Quarter is one of Basel's oldest districts and is home to several lesser-known art spaces and galleries. It offers a quiet, authentic atmosphere, with historical buildings and hidden art venues. The area is perfect for those seeking a more off-the-beaten-path experience in Basel. Many of the local galleries and artist studios in Klingental offer a more intimate viewing experience, showcasing both contemporary and classical works. Walking through this neighborhood allows you to connect with Basel's local art scene in a way that's different from the larger, more commercialized parts of the city. Estimated Price: Free to explore, gallery entry fees vary.

Lesser-Known Parks and Green Spaces

St. Alban-Tor Park

Located near the St. Alban district, St. Alban-Tor Park is a quiet, lesser-known green space that offers a peaceful retreat in the city. The park is set along the banks of the Rhine River and provides a beautiful view of the water and nearby historical buildings. It is less crowded compared to other parks in Basel, making it a perfect spot for relaxation, picnics, or a leisurely walk. The park is also close to the famous Basel Minster and is a hidden gem for those looking to escape the city's hustle and bustle.

Estimated Price: Free.

Merian Garten

Merian Garten is a botanical garden located a bit outside Basel's city center, but it offers a tranquil escape into nature. This spacious garden is home to a wide variety of plants, flowers, and trees, with themed sections such as a rose garden, an herb garden, and a tropical house. The garden also has a pond and a café, making it a relaxing place to spend a few hours. While well-known among locals, it's often overlooked by tourists, making it an excellent spot for those seeking a peaceful environment to explore Basel's flora.

Estimated Price: CHF 12 for adult entry.

Clarapark

Clarapark is a small, quiet park located in the Kleinbasel area. It's an ideal spot for a short break, with grassy areas perfect for lounging or picnicking. The park has several walking paths, a playground for children, and beautiful trees providing shade during the warmer months. Although not as large as other parks, Clarapark offers a more intimate green space experience.

It's a lovely place for locals to relax, and visitors looking for a peaceful retreat will appreciate its calm atmosphere.

Estimated Price: Free.

Bäumlihof Park

Bäumlihof Park is a hidden gem located in the northern part of Basel. It's a quiet neighborhood park with large green spaces, a small lake, and wooded areas, making it a perfect spot for walking, jogging, or simply enjoying nature. The park is less frequented by tourists, which adds to its charm and tranquility. It's a great place to relax away from the busy tourist areas, and it's a favorite among local residents for outdoor activities.

Estimated Price: Free.

Park im Grünen

Situated in the suburb of Riehen, Park im Grünen is a spacious park that offers a variety of outdoor activities. It features large lawns, tree-lined avenues, and beautiful walking paths. The park is also home to several sculptures and art installations, providing visitors with an opportunity to enjoy nature alongside art. It's not as crowded as some of Basel's central parks, making it a peaceful alternative for those looking for a quiet, scenic place to visit.

Estimated Price: Free.

Waidhalde Park

Waidhalde Park is located on the slopes of the Klein Basel district and offers stunning panoramic views of the city. It's a perfect spot for a relaxed stroll or a picnic, with plenty of space to unwind. The park is not heavily visited, offering a quieter atmosphere compared to more central locations. Waidhalde Park is particularly beautiful in the spring and summer months when the flowers and greenery are in full bloom. Estimated Price: Free.

Quiet Cafes and Unique Spots to Relax

Café des Arts

Located near the Kunstmuseum Basel, Café des Arts offers a peaceful, artistic atmosphere perfect for relaxing after a day of exploring museums and galleries. This café is a local favorite, known for its quiet setting and artistic ambiance. With comfortable seating and a laid-back vibe, it's a great spot to enjoy a coffee or pastry while admiring the art displayed on the walls. The café is often quieter than other spots in Basel, providing a perfect retreat for those looking to unwind. Estimated Price: Coffee from CHF 3-5, pastries from CHF 4-6.

Café Frühling

Café Frühling, located near the Basel SBB station, is a charming and cozy spot to relax and enjoy a warm drink. It offers a calm, inviting atmosphere with a simple yet elegant decor, and its outdoor seating area is particularly enjoyable during the warmer months. Café Frühling is known for its friendly service and quality coffee, making it a great place to relax, read, or simply people-watch. While it's not as tourist-heavy as other cafes in Basel, it remains a popular spot among locals.

Estimated Price: Coffee from CHF 3-5, sandwiches from CHF 7-10.

Café Papiermühle

Set inside the Basel Paper Mill Museum, Café Papiermühle offers a unique experience for visitors who want to enjoy a quiet drink surrounded by history. This hidden gem is ideal for those looking for a peaceful, almost meditative space to relax after exploring the museum. The café offers a selection of coffee, tea, and light snacks. Its location in a historical setting, combined with its serene atmosphere, makes it a perfect spot for unwinding in Basel's quieter, more off-the-beaten-path areas.

Estimated Price: Coffee from CHF 3-4, light snacks from CHF 5-7.

Kaffekommune

For coffee enthusiasts, Kaffekommune is a must-visit. Located in the St. Johanns-Vorstadt area, this specialty coffee shop offers expertly brewed coffee and a calm environment. The minimalist interior and quiet vibe make it an ideal location for spending a few hours relaxing or working on your laptop. Kaffekommune prides itself on its high-quality coffee and its dedication to sustainability, making it a great place to savor a cup while supporting local initiatives.
Estimated Price: Coffee from CHF 3-6, pastries from CHF 4-6.

Kunsthalle Basel Café

The café at Kunsthalle Basel provides a peaceful space for visitors to relax while enjoying views of the museum's exhibition spaces. With its quiet and contemporary design, the café serves a selection of coffee, tea, and light bites. It's a perfect spot to reflect on the exhibitions you've just seen or to take a break from your day of sightseeing. The café's laid-back atmosphere makes it a popular choice for those seeking a calm moment after exploring the art world in Basel.

Estimated Price: Coffee from CHF 3-5, light meals from CHF 7-12.

Erlenmattpark

Erlenmattpark, a quiet park located in the Kleinbasel area, is an excellent spot for relaxation away from the city's busy center. It is a large green space where locals often come to walk, sit, or read. The park features wide open spaces, shaded areas under trees, and a calm environment ideal for taking a break. Whether you're looking to enjoy a picnic or simply unwind in nature, Erlenmattpark offers a peaceful escape from the more crowded areas of Basel.

Estimated Price: Free.

The Cloisters of Basel Minster

For those seeking a tranquil and historic spot to relax, the cloisters of Basel Minster provide a serene environment with stunning views over the Rhine. This hidden area is often less crowded than the main parts of the cathedral and offers a peaceful space to sit and reflect. The architectural beauty of the cloisters, combined with the quiet ambiance, makes it a perfect place for meditation or simply taking a break from exploring the city.

Estimated Price: Free.

Rheinpromenade

The Rheinpromenade is a scenic riverside walk that stretches along the Rhine River, offering stunning views of Basel and the surrounding areas. It's a great spot to relax by the water, watch boats pass by, or enjoy a quiet moment in nature. The path is perfect for strolling or sitting on one of the benches located along the way. It's an ideal location for those seeking a peaceful, natural retreat within the city. Estimated Price: Free.

Nightlife and Entertainment

Basel's Vibrant Nightlife Scene

Understood! Here's a refined response with minimal bold text, only justified information, and using the preferred heading style.

Bars and Pubs

Basel is home to a variety of bars and pubs that cater to different crowds. Many of these are located in the Altstadt (Old Town) or along the Rhine River, offering a unique experience with both local and international drinks. Bars here offer everything from carefully crafted cocktails to diverse beer selections, making it a great spot for anyone looking to relax with a drink.

Nightclubs

Nightclubs in Basel offer a different vibe, with energetic environments centered around music. Popular clubs, such as "Prisma" and "Hafenklang," are known for electronic music and hosting international DJs. The city's nightlife has something for everyone, from those who enjoy deep house to those drawn to techno, making it one of Switzerland's more dynamic clubbing destinations.

Live Music

For music lovers, Basel offers plenty of live performances, whether it's a local indie band or a jazz ensemble. Venues like "Kaserne Basel" or "Gare du Nord" often showcase live acts that bring a diverse range of music genres to the city's nightlife scene, providing options for those looking for something beyond just dancing.

Cultural Venues

Cultural venues also contribute to Basel's vibrant night scene. The city's theaters, such as "Theatre Basel," offer late-night performances, while museums like the Kunsthalle Basel occasionally hold special events that combine art exhibitions with live music or performances, creating a unique way to spend an evening.

Rhine Promenade

For a more relaxed evening, Basel's Rhine Promenade is a popular option. Here, locals and visitors enjoy walking along the river, with several bars and cafes offering picturesque views. This makes for a more serene yet enjoyable way to spend time at night, with the added benefit of scenic surroundings.

Live Music Venues and Jazz Clubs

Live Music Venues in Basel

Basel is home to a variety of live music venues that cater to different tastes and styles. One of the city's standout locations for live performances is "Kaserne Basel." This venue offers an intimate setting, making it an ideal place to experience a wide range of music genres. It regularly hosts both local and international acts, featuring everything from indie bands to electronic music. The venue's small size allows for a personal, close-up experience, making it a popular choice for music enthusiasts who enjoy intimate performances.

Another well-regarded venue in Basel is "Gare du Nord." Known for its diverse musical programming, it offers a mixture of contemporary and traditional performances. The venue hosts a variety of acts, including rock concerts, acoustic performances, and experimental music. With its relaxed atmosphere and versatile stage, "Gare du Nord" provides a space for both established artists and emerging talents to showcase their work, making it a dynamic part of Basel's music scene.

Jazz Clubs in Basel

Jazz lovers will find plenty to enjoy in Basel, which is known for its thriving jazz scene. One of the most significant venues for jazz music in the city is "Jazzcampus Basel." As part of the Basel Jazz School, it serves as a central hub for both aspiring musicians and professional artists. The venue features regular performances, including concerts by students, faculty members, and visiting international jazz musicians. The laid-back atmosphere at Jazzcampus Basel makes it a great place for visitors to explore a wide variety of jazz styles, from traditional to more modern interpretations.

Another notable jazz venue in Basel is the "Bird's Eye Jazz Club." This cozy and intimate club is a favorite among locals and tourists alike, offering an excellent space for enjoying high-quality jazz performances. The club's intimate setting allows the audience to connect more closely with the performers, creating a rich and immersive experience. "Bird's Eye Jazz Club" regularly hosts both local talents and internationally renowned jazz artists, ensuring that every visit provides a fresh and exciting musical experience.

Evening Events and Festivals

Evening Events in Basel

Basel is home to a variety of evening events that cater to different interests throughout the year. One of the city's notable events is the **Basel Carnival**, which takes place annually in February or March. This vibrant festival, one of the largest in Europe, kicks off with the traditional "Morgestraich," where participants march through the streets in colorful costumes. The carnival continues for several days, featuring parades, music, and street performances. While the event is primarily a daytime celebration, the evening atmosphere, with illuminated processions and lively street parties, offers a unique experience for visitors.

For those looking for more cultural events, **Basel's Museum Night** is held annually, usually in the fall. This event allows visitors to explore the city's museums during extended hours, with many offering special exhibitions and performances. The event is a great opportunity to experience Basel's cultural scene after dark, as the city's museums host unique programs and activities for all ages.

Another popular evening event is the **Basel Light Festival**. Held every two years, this festival transforms Basel's streets and landmarks into a dazzling display of light art. Artists from around the world showcase their light installations, creating an immersive visual experience that brings the city to life at night.

Festivals in Basel

Basel hosts several major festivals throughout the year, making it a lively destination for visitors. **Art Basel**, the world-renowned contemporary art fair, takes place each June and brings together top galleries, artists, and collectors from around the world. While the fair itself is primarily a daytime event, Basel comes alive in the evening with related art exhibitions, parties, and performances.

Another significant event is **Basel's Christmas Market**, which starts in late November and continues through December. The market, one of the largest in Switzerland, features festive stalls offering local crafts, holiday treats, and mulled wine. In the evenings, the market is illuminated with festive lights, creating a magical atmosphere that draws both locals and tourists alike.

In the summer months, **Basel's Open-Air Theatre Festival** is a major draw. This festival, typically held in July and August, stages performances at various outdoor venues around the city. The festival includes a mix of theater, dance, and music, providing visitors with a chance to enjoy high-quality performances in the open air.

Late-Night Dining and Snacks

Late-Night Dining in Basel

Basel offers a variety of late-night dining options for those who prefer to enjoy a meal after typical restaurant hours. One popular choice is **Les Trois Rois**, a high-end restaurant that serves gourmet cuisine with a view of the Rhine River. While it's more well-known for its fine dining experience, it also offers late-night options, making it a go-to spot for those looking for a sophisticated meal after dark.

Another option for late-night dining is **Gifthüsli**, a traditional Swiss restaurant that remains open into the late evening. Offering hearty local dishes like fondue and raclette, this spot is perfect for those seeking comfort food after a long day of sightseeing or nightlife.

For a more casual experience, **Krafft Basel** offers both dining and drinks with a relaxed, welcoming atmosphere. Its menu includes a range of Swiss and international dishes, and the restaurant often stays open late, catering to guests who are still looking for a bite after a night out.

Late-Night Snacks in Basel

For those who just want a quick snack or bite to eat in the late hours, Basel has several places to consider. **Brasserie Les Trois Rois** offers a late-night bar menu with small plates, perfect for sharing with friends. Whether you're craving a light snack or a more filling option, this brasserie has a selection that can suit most tastes.

If you're looking for something even quicker, **Migros Take-Away** offers a range of pre-packaged snacks and sandwiches available at their late-night locations. This is an ideal option for those on the go, offering quick, accessible food without the wait.

For a more street food experience, **Basel's food trucks** are often scattered across the city in the evenings. These trucks typically serve fast, casual snacks, including burgers, fries, and kebabs. They're a great option for visitors looking for something tasty and convenient after a late night out.

Family-Friendly Activities

Fun for All Ages

Family-Friendly Activities in Basel

Basel offers a wide range of activities that are enjoyable for families with children. One of the top attractions is the **Zoo Basel**, Switzerland's oldest and one of the best-known zoos. Located in the heart of the city, the zoo is home to a variety of animals from around the world and offers educational exhibits and interactive activities that children can enjoy. The zoo's spacious grounds make it a pleasant place for families to spend the day, with areas designed specifically for children to learn and play.

Another popular family activity is a visit to the **Tinguely Museum**. This museum is dedicated to the works of Swiss artist Jean Tinguely, known for his kinetic art. The museum has interactive exhibits that engage children and encourage them to learn about art in a fun, hands-on way. It's a great spot for families to explore creativity and innovation.

For families who enjoy outdoor activities, **Kannenfeldpark** is a large green space in Basel that offers playgrounds, sports facilities, and plenty of room for picnics. The park's spacious layout and family-friendly atmosphere make it an ideal spot to relax and let children run around.

Educational Experiences for Children

Basel also offers educational activities that are both fun and informative for children. One such experience is a visit to the **Spielzeug Welten Museum**, a toy museum that showcases an extensive collection of toys from different time periods. The museum's exhibits include everything from dolls to miniature trains, and it offers a great way for children to learn about the history of play.

The **Basel Paper Mill Museum** provides another unique educational experience, where children can learn about the history of paper-making. The museum offers workshops where kids can make their own paper, providing both a hands-on learning experience and a fun activity.

River Activities

Families can also enjoy the **Rhine River** in Basel by taking a boat tour or even swimming during the summer months. The river is calm, and during the warmer weather, families can rent small boats or hop on a larger river cruise to take in the city's views from the water. Swimming in the river, known as **"Rhine Swimming,"** is a popular local pastime, and families can join in the fun at designated swimming areas.

Kid-Friendly Museums and Educational Spots

Kid-Friendly Museums in Basel

Basel has several museums that are both educational and fun for children. One of the most popular is the **Basel Toy Museum (Spielzeug Welten Museum)**. This museum houses a vast collection of toys, including dolls, teddy bears, and miniature trains, from various eras. The museum offers an interactive experience for children, allowing them to see how toys have evolved over the years. The colorful displays and hands-on exhibits make it an engaging visit for younger audiences.

Another great option is the **Natural History Museum Basel**. This museum is perfect for children interested in dinosaurs, animals, and the natural world. The museum features exhibits on fossils, wildlife, and Earth's geological history. Its interactive displays and educational programs are designed to capture the attention of young minds while also teaching them about the natural world.

For art-loving families, the **Kunsthalle Basel** offers exhibitions that can be interesting for children, with a variety of art installations and educational programs designed to make art accessible and fun for younger audiences. The museum occasionally holds workshops and events focused on children's art education.

Educational Spots for Kids

In addition to museums, Basel also has several educational spots that are both fun and informative for kids. The **Basel Paper Mill Museum** provides a hands-on experience where children can learn how paper was traditionally made. The museum offers interactive workshops where kids can try their hand at paper-making, giving them a deeper understanding of the process.

For families interested in science and technology, **Museum Tinguely** is another great option. It focuses on the works of Swiss artist Jean Tinguely, who created machines and kinetic sculptures. Many of the exhibits are interactive, allowing children to explore art and engineering in a playful way. The museum offers an educational experience that blends art with science, making it an exciting place for kids to visit.

Science and Nature Activities

For those interested in nature and science, the **Basel Zoo** is not just a place to see animals but also an educational experience.

The zoo offers various learning programs for children, teaching them about wildlife conservation, animal habitats, and biodiversity. The zoo's educational approach makes it an excellent spot for kids to learn about the animal kingdom in a fun, hands-on way.

Finally, **Kannenfeldpark**, with its large open spaces and natural environment, is another great spot for educational activities. The park provides opportunities for outdoor learning, with natural areas for exploration, picnic spots, and playgrounds. It's a perfect place for families to combine outdoor fun with informal education.

Parks and Playgrounds for Children

Parks for Children in Basel

Basel is home to several parks that are perfect for families and children to enjoy outdoor activities. One of the top choices is **Kannenfeldpark**, a large and spacious green area in the city. The park is equipped with playgrounds, open fields for running and sports, and plenty of shade for picnics. It's a great spot for families to spend the day outdoors, offering a relaxed environment where children can play freely.

Another popular park is **Gartenbad St. Jakob**, which combines a public swimming pool with a large outdoor area. The park is ideal for families who want to enjoy both water activities and open spaces. The pool is family-friendly, and the park offers plenty of room for children to play in a safe and controlled environment.

Schützenmattpark is another family-friendly option, located near the city center. This park features a playground with modern equipment, making it a popular spot for families with younger children. The park also has grassy areas for running, making it easy for kids to enjoy active play while parents relax.

Playgrounds for Children in Basel

Basel offers a variety of playgrounds scattered throughout the city, providing safe and fun spaces for children to enjoy. One standout is **Waidmarkt Playground**, located near the Basel City Hall. This well-maintained playground is equipped with swings, slides, and climbing structures that are suitable for children of different age groups. It's a great place for younger kids to burn off some energy while being in close proximity to the city's attractions.

The **Spielplatz Am See** playground, located near the Rhine River, offers a unique setting with a mix of traditional playground equipment and nature-inspired play areas. The scenic surroundings and proximity to the river make it an enjoyable spot for both kids and parents.

Another great playground is **Eisenbahnpark**, located near the Basel Train Station. This playground offers a variety of play structures and is particularly popular with younger children. Its location near other family-friendly attractions makes it a convenient stop for families exploring Basel.

Fun Outdoor Activities for Families

Outdoor Activities for Families in Basel

Basel offers a variety of outdoor activities that families can enjoy together. One of the most popular options is a visit to the **Rhine River**, where families can take part in several activities. During the warmer months, **Rhine swimming** is a favorite local activity. The river is calm, and there are designated areas where families can swim safely. Many locals enjoy swimming in the river, which is a fun and unique way for families to experience the city.

Another great outdoor activity is a **bike ride along the Rhine**. Basel has an extensive network of bike paths, and families can rent bikes to explore the city and its surroundings. A bike ride along the river offers beautiful views of Basel's architecture and green spaces, making it a pleasant and scenic way to spend the day. You can stop at various parks and cafés along the way for breaks, making it a relaxed family outing.

For a more active outdoor experience, **hiking in the nearby hills** is another excellent option. The area around Basel offers several hiking trails suitable for families, ranging from easy walks to more challenging hikes. The **Basel-Münsterberg** hill provides beautiful panoramic views of the city, and the nearby **Jurapark** offers additional hiking opportunities surrounded by nature, perfect for families looking to connect with the outdoors.

Parks and Open Spaces for Family Fun

As mentioned earlier, **Kannenfeldpark** is a spacious park that caters to families with its playgrounds, open fields, and picnic areas. This park is perfect for a day of outdoor fun, offering a variety of activities like playing frisbee, flying kites, or just relaxing while children enjoy the swings and slides.

Gartenbad St. Jakob is another excellent spot for families who want to combine outdoor play with swimming. With its large park and swimming pool, families can spend the day relaxing, playing, and cooling off in the water. It's especially ideal for families with younger children who enjoy both playtime in the park and water-based activities.

If your family enjoys sports, **Schützenmattpark** offers various sports facilities, including a basketball court, tennis courts, and areas for soccer and other games. The playground is well-equipped for children, and the spacious fields provide ample room for active play.

Family-Friendly Boat Tours

Another fun outdoor activity for families is a **boat tour along the Rhine**. These tours offer a unique perspective of the city, allowing families to see Basel's landmarks from the water. Many boat tours are family-friendly, offering comfortable seating and scenic views, making it a relaxing yet enjoyable activity for families of all ages.

Family-Friendly Dining Options

Family-Friendly Dining in Basel

Basel offers several family-friendly dining options that cater to both adults and children. One great option is **Restaurant Gasthof zum. Pschorr**, a traditional Swiss restaurant known for its warm, welcoming atmosphere. The restaurant offers a variety of classic Swiss dishes like fondue and rösti, as well as a kids' menu with options that children will enjoy. The relaxed, casual setting makes it an excellent choice for families looking for a comfortable meal.

Another family-friendly spot is **Klara**, a modern café that offers both a cozy atmosphere and a menu with a variety of healthy and kid-friendly dishes. The café's offerings range from fresh salads to sandwiches and soups, making it an ideal location for families with younger children or picky eaters. Its location near the city center also makes it a convenient stop for families after a day of sightseeing.

Restaurant Dampfzentrale is another family-friendly venue located along the Rhine River. It has a large outdoor seating area, allowing families to enjoy their meals while overlooking the river. The menu is diverse, with options for both adults and children, including kid-sized portions of local Swiss dishes and international favorites. The relaxed environment makes it perfect for families who want to enjoy a meal without the rush.

Kid-Friendly Menus and Special Dining Events

Several restaurants in Basel offer dedicated kids' menus designed to appeal to younger tastes. For example, **Café des Arts** in the heart of Basel offers a wide range of meals suitable for kids, such as pasta, chicken nuggets, and freshly made pizzas. The restaurant's relaxed atmosphere, combined with the kid-friendly menu, makes it a go-to choice for families with young children.

On weekends, **Basilisk Restaurant** hosts special family-friendly events, such as brunch buffets with a variety of child-friendly foods. This dining spot is designed with families in mind, offering a kid-friendly environment where children can enjoy their meals while parents relax.

Outdoor Dining for Families

For families who prefer outdoor dining, **Rhine Promenade** is home to several restaurants and cafés with outdoor seating. These venues offer a family-friendly experience, with casual menus that include burgers, fries, sandwiches, and more. Dining along the river allows families to enjoy the fresh air and views of Basel while having a relaxed meal.

Day Trips and Attractions Suitable for Families

Day Trips from Basel

Basel's central location makes it a great starting point for family-friendly day trips. One of the most popular options is a visit to **Lausanne**, located about an hour and a half from Basel by train. This city on the shores of Lake Geneva offers plenty of family-friendly attractions, including the **Olympic**

Museum, where children can learn about the history of the Olympic Games through interactive exhibits. Families can also enjoy a boat ride on the lake or visit the nearby **Château de Chillon**, a medieval castle that offers a fascinating exploration experience for kids and adults alike.

Another great day trip is to **Lucerne**, about an hour and a half by train from Basel. Known for its stunning lake and mountain views, Lucerne offers attractions like the **Swiss Transport Museum**, which features hands-on exhibits about trains, planes, and automobiles, perfect for children interested in transportation. The **Kapellbrücke (Chapel Bridge)** and **Lion Monument** are also top spots for families, offering a mix of history and outdoor exploration.

Families interested in nature can head to **Jura Park**, about an hour's drive from Basel. The park offers opportunities for hiking, wildlife spotting, and enjoying the outdoors. Children can explore the natural surroundings, visit educational exhibits, and even participate in interactive activities about the environment.

Attractions in Basel for Families

For families staying in Basel, there are numerous attractions that are both fun and educational. The **Basel Zoo** is one of the oldest zoos in Switzerland and home to a wide range of animals from around the world. It's an ideal place for children to learn about wildlife and conservation, with special programs and events designed for young visitors.

The **Kunstmuseum Basel** offers a more cultural experience for families. While art museums can sometimes feel inaccessible for children, the museum's educational programs and family-friendly tours help kids engage with the exhibits. The museum's collection includes works from famous artists, providing a great opportunity for children to explore art in a fun and interactive way.

The **Tinguely Museum** in Basel is another family-friendly attraction. The museum is dedicated to the works of Swiss artist Jean Tinguely, known for his kinetic sculptures. The interactive nature of many of the exhibits, which allow children to touch and explore the art, makes it an engaging visit for families.

Another family favorite is the **Basel Paper Mill Museum**, where children can learn about the history of paper-making. The museum offers workshops where kids can create their own paper, providing an educational yet hands-on experience.

Finally, families can spend time at **Kannenfeldpark**, a large green space in Basel that offers playgrounds, open fields, and picnic areas. It's an ideal spot for kids to burn off some energy, and parents can relax while enjoying the park's peaceful surroundings.

Day Trips from Basel

Best Nearby Destinations for a Day Trip

Nearby Destinations for a Day Trip from Basel

Basel's central location near the borders of Switzerland, France, and Germany makes it an excellent starting point for a variety of day trips. Here are some of the best nearby destinations that are ideal for a family day trip.

Colmar, France

Located just an hour's drive from Basel, **Colmar** is a picturesque town in the Alsace region of France, known for its charming medieval architecture and colorful half-timbered houses. The **Old Town** is particularly family-friendly, with cobblestone streets, beautiful canals, and the **Unterlinden Museum**, which offers an engaging mix of art and history for all ages. Families can also enjoy a boat ride along the canals, offering a relaxing way to take in the scenery.

Mulhouse, France

Just a 30-minute drive from Basel, **Mulhouse** is home to the **Cité de l'Automobile**, one of the largest automobile museums in the world. This museum features an extensive collection of vintage cars, providing a great opportunity for children to learn about the history of automobiles in an interactive and engaging way. Mulhouse is also home to the **Cité du Train**, a railway museum that's perfect for train enthusiasts of all ages.

Lucerne, Switzerland

About an hour and a half by train from Basel, **Lucerne** is a beautiful city nestled on the shores of Lake Lucerne and surrounded by the Swiss Alps. The **Swiss Museum of Transport** is a highlight for families, offering interactive exhibits about trains, planes, and automobiles. Families can also explore the **Chapel Bridge**, the **Lion Monument**, and take a boat trip on the lake, offering plenty of opportunities for outdoor activities.

Lake Constance, Germany

Around an hour and a half's drive from Basel, **Lake Constance** (Bodensee) is a stunning area that stretches across Germany, Austria, and Switzerland. The lake offers numerous family-friendly activities, such as boat tours, cycling around the shoreline, and exploring towns like **Friedrichshafen**, which is home to the **Zeppelin Museum**, a fun and educational stop for families. The area is also known for its beautiful parks, making it a great place for a picnic or a leisurely walk.

Zurich, Switzerland

Just an hour by train from Basel, **Zurich** is a vibrant city that offers a variety of family-friendly activities. Families can visit the **Zurich Zoo**, which features an impressive collection of animals and a unique Masoala Rainforest exhibit. The **Swiss National Museum** offers interactive displays that can capture the interest of younger visitors, and a stroll along **Lake Zurich** provides a relaxing way to enjoy the scenic surroundings.

Baden, Switzerland

Less than an hour by train from Basel, **Baden** is a small spa town that offers a peaceful escape with its beautiful parks and historic sites. The town is known for its natural hot springs, and families can visit the **Felsenegg** trail for stunning views of the surrounding area. Baden also features several museums, such as the **Roman Baths Museum**, which provides insight into the town's history as a Roman spa destination.

Exploring the Countryside and Nearby Villages

Exploring the Countryside Around Basel

The area surrounding Basel offers plenty of opportunities to explore the Swiss countryside and nearby villages. These regions provide a mix of natural beauty, charming villages, and outdoor activities that are perfect for a day trip.

One of the best ways to experience the countryside is by visiting the **Basel-Landschaft** region, just a short distance from the city. This area is known for its scenic landscapes, including rolling hills, vineyards, and forests. Families can enjoy walking or cycling along various trails that wind through picturesque villages and offer stunning views of the Swiss Jura Mountains. The village of **Liestal** is a great starting point for exploring the region, offering easy access to hiking trails and historical sites, such as the **Liestal Castle**.

The **Kaiseraugst** area, near Basel, is another excellent place to visit. Here, you can explore the **Augusta Raurica**, an ancient Roman archaeological site that includes well-preserved ruins and a museum. The surrounding countryside provides plenty of green space for picnics and leisurely walks, making it a family-friendly destination.

Nearby Villages to Explore

For those looking to explore Swiss village life, the villages of **Riehen** and **St. Johann** are ideal destinations. Both are located near Basel and offer a peaceful escape from the city. **Riehen** is known for its rural charm, offering easy access to the **Vitra Design Museum** and the **Schloss Riehen** (Riehen Castle). The village is surrounded by green spaces, making it perfect for a family walk or bike ride.

St. Johann is another nearby village that provides a blend of history and nature. The village is home to several traditional Swiss houses and offers views of the **Basel countryside**. Families can enjoy a leisurely walk through the village or explore the nearby **Waidbachtal**, a scenic valley that's perfect for hiking.

Vineyards and Wine Tours

The regions surrounding Basel are also known for their vineyards. The **Basel-Territory Wine Route** offers an opportunity to explore Swiss wine culture, with several vineyards located in the surrounding hills and valleys. Families can enjoy a visit to one of these vineyards, learn about the winemaking process, and even sample local wines. Some vineyards offer guided tours that include a walk through the vineyards, making it an educational and enjoyable experience for all ages.

The **Thierstein** and **Aargau** areas are particularly famous for their vineyards, and a visit to these regions provides a chance to explore the countryside while enjoying views of grapevines stretching across the hills. These areas also offer several walking and cycling paths, allowing families to enjoy the outdoors while discovering the local wine culture.

Adventure and Nature Day Trips from Basel

The region around Basel offers a variety of adventure and nature day trips, ideal for those looking to explore the outdoors and experience Switzerland's stunning landscapes. Here are some of the best options for families and outdoor enthusiasts:

Jura Mountains

The **Jura Mountains**, located just a short drive from Basel, offer plenty of opportunities for outdoor adventure. This range is perfect for hiking, with numerous trails suitable for families, from easy walks to more challenging hikes. The area offers scenic views, forests, and small villages that can be explored on foot. During the winter months, the Jura region is a popular destination for skiing and snowshoeing, making it an ideal place for year-round outdoor activities. One of the highlights of the Jura Mountains is **Mont Tendre**, the highest point in the region, offering panoramic views of the surrounding area.

Kandersteg and Oeschinen Lake

About a two-hour drive from Basel, **Kandersteg** is a popular destination for nature lovers. The village is surrounded by towering mountains and lush forests, and it serves as a gateway to **Oeschinen Lake**, a stunning alpine lake known for its clear, turquoise waters. Families can enjoy a scenic cable car ride to the lake, followed by a hike along the shore or a boat ride on the lake. The area also offers various outdoor activities, such as swimming, fishing, and picnicking, making it an ideal spot for a full day of adventure in nature.

Black Forest, Germany

A little over an hour's drive from Basel, the **Black Forest** in Germany offers a range of outdoor activities for nature enthusiasts. The region is known for its dense forests, picturesque villages, and hiking trails. Families can explore the **Schluchsee**, a large lake that offers swimming, paddle boating, and hiking around the shores. The **Triberg Waterfalls** are another popular natural attraction, with a well-maintained trail that leads visitors through lush forest to view the tallest waterfalls in Germany. The Black Forest is also known for its traditional villages, where visitors can learn about the region's rich cultural heritage.

Rheinfall (Rhine Falls) Located about an hour from Basel, **Rheinfall** is Europe's largest waterfall, located near the town of **Schaffhausen**. The falls are a stunning natural spectacle, with water flowing over a 150-meter-wide rock face. Families can explore the area via boat tours that take you up close to the falls, or visit the viewing platforms for breathtaking views. The surrounding area offers walking trails, gardens, and picnic spots, making it a great place for a family outing.

Swiss National Park

For a more remote adventure, the **Swiss National Park** near Zernez, about two and a half hours from Basel, offers an authentic experience of Switzerland's alpine wilderness. The park is home to a variety of wildlife, including ibex, marmots, and golden eagles, and offers a network of well-marked trails suitable for different levels of hiking. This park is one of Switzerland's oldest national parks and offers families the chance to experience nature in its purest form, surrounded by dramatic mountain scenery and untouched forests.

River Cruises and Scenic Train Routes

Basel is well-situated along the **Rhine River**, making it an excellent starting point for river cruises. The **Rhine River Cruises** offer a relaxing and scenic way to explore the surrounding areas. One popular option is a **day cruise** that takes you along the river to picturesque towns such as **Koblenz** in Germany or **Strasbourg** in France. These cruises typically offer panoramic views of the riverbanks, charming villages, and castles, making it a great way for families to experience the beauty of the Rhine without needing to rush through multiple destinations.

For a more immersive experience, families can opt for multi-day cruises that go further along the Rhine, offering more opportunities to visit historical cities like **Cologne** or **Amsterdam**. Many river cruise lines provide family-friendly amenities and excursions, including shore trips to local attractions, museums, and scenic walking tours.

Another great option is a **local boat tour** in Basel itself. Several companies offer guided boat trips along the Rhine, where you can explore the city from the water. This is a relaxing way to take in the sights of Basel, with commentary about the city's history and landmarks, such as the **Kunstmuseum Basel** and **Basel Minster**. These shorter cruises are ideal for families who want to see the city from a different perspective.

Scenic Train Routes from Basel

Basel's central location in Switzerland allows for easy access to several scenic train routes, offering a chance to experience the country's stunning landscapes by rail.

Glacier Express

One of Switzerland's most famous scenic train routes, the **Glacier Express**, runs from **Zermatt** to **St. Moritz**. The journey is around eight hours long, but it's well worth the time for the breathtaking views of the Swiss Alps. Families can relax in panoramic windows, enjoying the stunning scenery of mountain passes, deep valleys, and alpine lakes. The Glacier

Express is known for its luxury service, making it a comfortable and unforgettable way to see Switzerland's mountainous regions.

Bernina Express

The **Bernina Express** is another world-renowned scenic train route that travels between **Chur** and **Tirano** in Italy, passing through the **Swiss Alps**. This route is particularly spectacular because it crosses the **Bernina Range**, offering incredible views of glaciers, deep valleys, and high-altitude landscapes. The train travels through the **Alp Grüm**, where families can take in the panoramic views of snow-capped peaks and glacial lakes. This scenic journey is one of the most unique in Europe, combining nature with impressive engineering feats like the **Landwasser Viaduct**.

GoldenPass Line

For a shorter, but equally scenic route, the **GoldenPass Line** connects **Montreux** on Lake Geneva to **Gstaad**, offering views of Swiss lakes, charming villages, and the surrounding mountains. This train ride is an excellent choice for families who want to experience the beauty of the Swiss countryside without committing to a full-day journey. The GoldenPass Line offers several different segments, so you can choose the section that best suits your time and interests.

Exploring Neighboring Countries

Exploring Germany from Basel

Basel's location near the borders of Germany makes it easy to explore nearby German cities and attractions. One popular destination is **Freiburg**, a vibrant city located about an hour's drive from Basel. Freiburg is known for its medieval architecture, including the **Freiburg Minster**, a stunning

Gothic cathedral. The city's **Altstadt (Old Town)** is also worth exploring, with narrow streets, quaint shops, and local cafés. Freiburg is also a great base for exploring the **Black Forest**, offering a variety of outdoor activities such as hiking, cycling, and scenic drives.

Another great destination in Germany is **Heidelberg**, approximately an hour and a half from Basel by car or train. The city is home to the **Heidelberg Castle**, which overlooks the town and offers spectacular views. The **Old Bridge** and the historic **Altstadt** are also top attractions, making Heidelberg a popular choice for those interested in history and culture.

For a more modern experience, **Karlsruhe**, located about an hour from Basel, offers a mix of contemporary culture and historical landmarks. The **Zoological City Garden** and **Karlsruhe Palace** are among the city's highlights, providing a pleasant combination of green spaces and historical sites.

Exploring France from Basel

Basel's proximity to France also offers visitors the chance to explore several fascinating French destinations. **Colmar**, located about an hour's drive from Basel, is one of the most picturesque towns in the Alsace region. Known for its colorful half-timbered houses, cobblestone streets, and canals, Colmar offers a unique and charming atmosphere. The **Unterlinden Museum** in Colmar is home to a famous altarpiece and other art collections, making it a great stop for culture lovers.

Another destination in France worth visiting is **Strasbourg**, located just over an hour from Basel. Strasbourg is famous for its **Notre-Dame Cathedral**, a stunning example of Gothic architecture, and its picturesque **La Petite France** district, known for its traditional timber-framed houses. The **European Parliament** building is also located in Strasbourg, making it an interesting stop for those interested in European politics.

For those interested in wine and food, **Riquewihr**, also in the Alsace region, is a small village that offers a more rural experience. Located just under an hour from Basel, Riquewihr is surrounded by vineyards and is known for its local wines, which can be tasted at various wine cellars in the area.

Day Trips from Basel to Germany and France

Basel is ideally located for day trips to both Germany and France, offering visitors the opportunity to explore the culture, food, and landscapes of these neighboring countries in a short amount of time. Whether you're visiting the medieval towns of Germany or exploring the vineyards of France, the ease of travel between these countries makes Basel an excellent base for cross-border exploration.

Conclusion

Basel's blend of medieval charm and contemporary flair exemplifies Switzerland's love of both tradition and innovation. From the iconic red-sandstone Minster and centuries-old Old Town alleys to modern art galleries and sleek riverside developments, the city balances past and present in a way that feels effortlessly welcoming. Whether strolling along the Rhine, exploring its dynamic cultural institutions, or savoring local favorites in a historic square, you'll discover that Basel rewards the curious traveler with hidden corners and friendly encounters at every turn. By immersing yourself in Basel's rich heritage, trying new tastes and experiences, and taking the time to engage with its multifaceted neighborhoods, you'll leave not only with photographs of picturesque architecture but with a deeper appreciation for a city that confidently bridges history and modern life. As you depart, may your memories of Basel's vibrant markets, world-class museums, and inviting café terraces inspire you to return— ready to uncover even more of this fascinating destination.

Printed in Dunstable, United Kingdom

64851309R00087